BY SARAH RUTHERFORD

FIRST PERFORMED AT
TRAFALAGAR STUDIOS, LONDON 15 OCTOBER 2019

Cast

THEA – Claire Goose
GIL – Navin Chowdhry
BILLIE – Rosie Day
LENNY – Will Fletcher

Creative

Writer – Sarah Rutherford
Director – Hannah Price
Producer – Eilene Davidson
Set Designer – Georgia De Grey
Lighting Designer – Robbie Butler
Sound Designer – Adrienne Quartly
Production Manager – Production Manager
Costume Associate – Zahra Mansouri
Stage Manager – Maria Colette Buckley
Casting Director – Ellie Collyer-Bristow

Claire Goose

Claire Goose's theatre credits include: *Holy Sh!t* (Kiln Theatre); *Twitstorm* (Cahoots Theatre Company); *The Perfect Murder* (Theatre Royal Bath); *When We Were Rich* (Southampton Nuffield Theatre); *Addicted to Love* (Bristol Old Vic) and *Hitting Home* (the Man in the Moon Theatre).

Television credits include: *Dark Heart* (ITV); *Lucky Man* (Carnival); *The Coroner* (BBC); *Death in Paradise* (BBC); *New Tricks* (BBC); *Mount Pleasant* (Sky); *Undeniable* (TXTV); *Exile* (BBC); *Hustle* (BBC); *The Bill* (Talkback Thames); *Perfect Day* (Channel 5); *Love Lies Bleeding* (ITV); *Secret Smile* (Granada Television); *The Good Citizen* (BBC); *Gifted* (ITV) and *Walking the Dead*, *Casualty*, *EastEnders*, *Landmarks* and *Loved Up* (BBC).

Film credits include: *Generation Z*, *Candle to Water*, *Bad Day*, *Friday Night In*, *Danny Loves Angela* and *Meat*.

Navin Chowdhry

Navin Chowdhry has starred in a number of award-winning TV shows, including *The End of the F***ing World* (Channel 4) and *A Touch of Cloth* (ITV). Last year, he shot *Our Girl* (BBC) and is currently filming *Invisible* (ITV). Navin also starred in the BBC's BAFTA Award-winning *Doctor Foster* and *The Replacement*.

His theatre credits include: *Multitudes* (Tricycle Theatre); *Much Ado About Nothing* (The Globe) and *Behind the Image and Shades* (Royal Court), which picked up an Evening Standard Award.

Other credits include: the critically acclaimed *Teachers*, *Next of Kin*, *The Job Lot* and *Babylon*.

Rosie Day

Rosie Day, a Screen International Star of Tomorrow, can be seen as the young female lead in new comedy drama *Living the Dream* for Big Talk/Sky and will next be seen in indie feature *Butterfly Kisses* (winner of the Crystal Bear Award at this year's Berlin Film Festival). Last year, Rosie played one of the leads in Rodrigo Cortés' *Down a Dark Hall* alongside Uma Thurman and was seen in Starz' blockbuster TV series *Outlander – series two*.

Other notable credits include: *All Roads Lead to Rome* alongside Sarah Jessica Parker, *The Heretiks*, *The Seasoning House*, *Ironclad: Battle for Blood* and *Sixteen*.

Other television credits include: *Cuffs*, *Homefront* and *Misfits*.

Will Fletcher

Will Fletcher began his training at RADA and went on to study at Bristol Old Vic Theatre School and graduated with a BA in Professional Acting in 2019.

Theatre credits include: *Let the Right One In*, *Poison*, *The Life and Adventures of Nicholas Nickleby*, *Sam Wanamaker Festival*, *Beowulf* (Theatre In Education Tour); *The Mill on the Floss* (West Country tour); *The Railway Children*, *A View From the Bridge*, *Philistines*, *The Importance of Being Earnest*, *Twelfth Night* and *Lungs* (all performed with the Bristol Old Vic Theatre School) and *Macbeth* (RADA).

Sarah Rutherford – Writer

Sarah Rutherford was the inaugural writer in residence of Park Theatre, where her play *Adult Supervision* was nominated Best Off-West End Production at the WhatsOnStage Awards.

Born in Scotland, she has a first class degree in English from Oxford University and completed a PhD at Edinburgh University on *Black Farce in Jacobean* and *1960s Theatre* while working as a freelance journalist and broadcaster. She then trained at Guildford School of Acting and worked as an actor for over a decade before becoming a playwright and screenwriter. Sarah is currently under commission to feminist theatre company Scary Little Girls, and other plays include *Hybrid Vigour*, *In Neon* and *What You Do to People*. She has also worked on research and development projects and readings at the National Theatre, Royal Shakespeare Company, Donmar Warehouse, Hampstead Theatre, Theatre Royal Stratford East and Leeds Playhouse. She is now working on a number of film and TV projects, and is one half of 2not2 Productions with actor Tanya Moodie.

Eilene Davidson – Producer and Co-artistic Director of Stage Traffic

Eilene is an international theatre producer who has worked in the USA, UK and Europe.

Recent produced plays include: *War Paint* (Nederlander Theatre, Broadway, 2017); *Fraulein Julie* (Schmidt Theatre, Hamburg, 2017); *The Grinning Man* (Trafalgar Studios, London, 2017–18); *Monogamy* (Park Theatre, London, and UK tour, 2018); *Consent* (Pinter Theatre, London, 2018); *Dusty* with Eleanor Lloyd (UK tour); *Paper Dolls* (Mosaic Theatre, Washington, USA, 2018); *Misty* (Trafalgar Studios, London, October/November 2018); *Pinter season* (Pinter Theatre, London, 2018/19); *Emilia* (Vaudeville Theatre, 2019); *Admissions* (Trafalgar Studio, 2019); *Caroline's Kitchen* (59E59 Theatres, NYC); *The Starry Messenger* (Wyndham's Theatre, summer 2019); *On Your Feet* (Leicester Curve, London Coliseum and UK tour, 2019/20); *Betrayal* (Broadway, NYC) and *9 to 5* (Savoy Theatre, London, 2019/20). She is also currently producing *A Day in the Death of Joe Egg* in Studio 1 at Trafalgar Studios. In 2016, Eilene set up Stage Traffic to exclusively showcase new writing in the States and UK.

Recently acclaimed productions include: *This Little Life of Mine* (Park Theatre); *Late Company* and *3 Women* (Trafalgar Studios) and *Spiro, Spero* (Calderwood Pavilion, Boston, USA). Eilene formerly worked as an actress, writer and dramaturg in USA/UK and is on the board of the prestigious Huntington Theatre in Boston, USA.

Hannah Price – Director

Hannah is Co-artistic Director and founder of Theatre Uncut, the winner of two Fringe First Awards, a Herald Angel award and the Spirit of the Fringe Award. She has directed for theatre, television and video games.

Theatre includes: *End of the Pier* (Park Theatre); *Down and Out in Paris* and *London Live* (Stone Nest/La Galeries); *Again* (Trafalgar Studios); *Permanence* (Tarragon Theatre, Toronto); *Escape the Scaffold* (Theatre503 and the Other Room); *Run the Beast Down* (Marlowe Theatre/Finborough); *1984 Live* (Senate House); *Rainbow Class* (Bush Theatre/ Assembly Rooms); *TEST* (Scala Theatre, Basel); *The Dead Monkey* (Park Theatre); *Boa* (Trafalgar Studios); *Cello/ Fragile* (Yard Theatre) and *Bud Take the Wheel I Feel a Song Coming On* (Shaw Theatre/Underbelly). For Theatre Uncut: *Refugee* (Teater Grob, Copenhagen); *In Opposition* (Paines Plough Roundabout); *Knowledge Is Power: Knowledge Is Change* (Traverse/national tour); *Referendum Plays* (Traverse); *Power and Protest* (Dot Tiyatro, Istanbul/Traverse); *The Rise of the Right (Young Vic)* and *The Cuts Plays* (Southwark Playhouse, Soho Theatre, Latitude Festival and Traverse).

Georgia De Grey – Set Designer

Georgia is an award-winning, freelance designer for theatre, opera and dance. She was a finalist for the Linbury Prize for Stage Design in 2013 and was nominated for an Off West End Theatre Award for her set design for *Alkaline* at the Park Theatre.

Recent credits include: *Rails* by Simon Longman (Theatre by the Lake); *The Listening Room* by Harriet Madley (UK tour/Theatre Royal Stratford East); *The Noises* by Jaqueline Saphra, *One Jewish Boy* by Stephen Laughton *and Birthday Suit* by David K Barnes (Old Red Lion Theatre); *Alkaline* by Stephanie Martin (Park Theatre); *Our Town* by Thornton Wilder and *Spring Storm* by Tennessee Williams (North Wall Arts Centre); *If We Got Some More Cocaine I Could Show You How I Love You* by John O'Donovan (Project Arts Theatre, Dublin, and tour/Old Red Lion Theatre); *Superhero* by Richy Hughes, Joseph Finlay and Michael Conley (Southwark Playhouse); *Incident at Vichy* by Arthur Miller (Finborough Theatre); *Erwartung* by Arnold Schoenberg and *Twice Through the Heart* by Mark Anthony Turnage (Hackney Showroom); *Sister* by Alex Groves and Rebecca Hanbury (Spitalfields Music Festival and Ovalhouse Theatre); *Best Served Cold* by Cordelia Lynn *(Vault Festival)* and *The Last Days of Mankind* (Bristol Old Vic).

Robbie Butler – Lighting Designer

Robbie trained at the Royal Conservatoire of Scotland. He is an honorary life member of the Association of Lighting Designers, has twice been nominated for an Off West End Theatre Award for Best Lighting Design and was the winner of the 2015 ETC Award.

Theatre includes: *Mushy: Lyrically Speaking* (Watford Palace Theatre and UK tour); *A Prayer for Wings* (Volcano Theatre, Swansea); *The Guards at the Taj*, *My Mother Said I Never Should* and *The Children* (Theatre by the Lake, Keswick); *Oral* (regional tour); *The Crown Dual* (King's Head and Edinburgh Festival Fringe); *The Happy Tragedy of Being Woke* (Complicité/Edinburgh International Festival); *The Wonderful Wizard of Oz* (Macron Stadium, Bolton); *The Selfish Giant* (UK tour); *Down and Out: Live* (La Generale, Paris); *Lady Macwata* (Ghostlight Theatre Co); *Abandoman* (Underbelly Productions); *For King and Country* (Southwark Playhouse); *There or Here* (Park Theatre); *The Wind in the Willows* (Core Theatre); *Mother Courage and Her Children* (Southwark Playhouse); *Run the Beast Down* (Marlowe Theatre); as well as many productions at the Finborough Theatre, the Old Red Lion Theatre, and Brighton and Edinburgh fringe festivals.

Opera includes: *Isabeau* (Opera Holland Park); *Dialogues des Carmélites* (Guildhall School); *Il trovatore* (the Royal Danish Opera and Teatro Real, Madrid – associate) and *The Enchanted Pig* (HGO).

For more, visit robbiebutlerdesigns.com

Adrienne Quartly – Sound Designer

Adrienne is a sound designer/composer for theatre. Her work has been presented all over the world.

Recent shows include: *Citysong* (Abbey Theatre, Dublin); *Queen Margaret* (Royal Exchange, Manchester); *The Paper Man* (Improbable Theatre); *Black Men Walking* (Royal Court Theatre); *Kindertransport* and *The Crucible* (Les Théâtres de la Ville de Luxembourg); *Get Happy* (Beijing Comedy Festival); *Opening Skinner's Box* (Lincoln Center Festival, New York); *A Tale of Two Cities* (Royal & Derngate, Northampton); *Bad Jews* (Theatre Royal Haymarket); *I Am Thomas* (Told by an Idiot/NTS); *Splendour* (Donmar Warehouse); *The Ghost Train* (Told by an Idiot); *Inside Wagner's Head* (Royal Opera House); *Frauline Julie* (Schaubühne, Berlin/Barbican); *Rings of Saturn* (AbenteuerHallenKalk, Cologne) and *Thomas Hobbes* and *Mary Schindler* (RSC). Adrienne was part of the team behind the Olivier-nominated production of *Cuttin' It* (Young Vic Theatre – Best New Play nomination at the UK Theatre Awards); *Black Men Walking* (Eclipse) and Best Production at the Manchester Theatre Awards for Rose (Home).

For more, visit adriennequartly.com.

Sarah Reed – Production Manager

Sarah has over 15 years' experience in stage management, marketing and theatre administration. She is privileged to have worked on all Stage Traffic's shows, including *This Little Life of Mine* (Park Theatre); *Late Company* (Finborough Theatre and Trafalgar Studios); 3 *Women* (Trafalgar Studios) and production-managed for *A Guide for the Homesick* and *The Girl Who Fell* (both Trafalgar Studios).

Recent credits include: special events for *Emilia* (Vaudeville Theatre), including the successful *Women Celebrating Women* evening, and tour booking for Theatre Tours International.

Training includes: BA (hons) Politics, Philosophy and Economics (the Open University) and a PGCert in Management and Finance (London School of Business and Finance). Sarah has recently completed the highly regarded Stage One Workshop for new producers.

Zahra Mansouri – Costumer Associate

Zahra Mansouri graduated in 2009 from Central Saint Martins in BA (hons) Design for Performance. She has been nominated twice by the Off West End Theatre Awards and has been the associate designer at Fourth Monkey Theatre School for nine years, reaching show 75. Up-and-coming design work: *Goldilocks and the Three Musketeers* (BAC) and Kiln Cinema immersive experience.

Recent work: *Typical* (Soho Theatre); *Valhalla with Geko Theatre* (Camden Fringe); as costume designer for *Dead Man Walking* (Oldenburgisches Staatstheater) and set and costume for site-specific opera Nazzar the Brave (Armenian Opera Company).

Other work includes: *3 Women and Late Company* (Trafalgar Studios 2); *Movie Trilogy* (Royal Albert Hall Studio); *Orlando* (Knole House with BFI Flare); *The Great Gatsby* (Wilton's Music Hall); *This Little Life of Mine* and *The American Wife* (Park Theatre 90); *Finding Butterfly* (Limehouse Town Hall); *The Marked* (Ovalhouse) and *The Cause* (Jermyn Street Theatre).

As costume associate/supervisor: *The Trench* (Southwark Playhouse); *Inside Pussy Riot (Saatchi Gallery)* and *The Toxic Avenger* (Arts Theatre).

For more, visit: zahramansouri.com.

Maria Colette Buckley – Stage Manager

Training: stage management and technical theatre at London Academy of Music and Dramatic Arts.

Recent credits include: assistant stage manager for *Cat on a Hot Tin Roof* (Young Vic); ASM cover for *Cinderella* at the London Palladium (Qdos Entertainment); production runner for *Barnum* UK tour (Cameron Mackintosh Productions) and *Hamlet* (Michael Attenborough).

Stage management placements include: UK tour of *Grease* (David Ian Productions) and *Who's Afraid of Virginia Woolf?* (Sonia Friedman Productions). LAMDA productions include: *Hobson's Choice* (deputy stage manager); *The Sea* (stage manager); *Birdy* (technical stage manager) and *A Midsummer Night's Dream* (assistant stage manager). Maria also received scholarships from the Andrew Lloyd Webber Foundation and Zoë Dominic Foundation helping to fund her training at LAMDA. This is Maria's first time working with Stage Traffic and she's so excited be a part of this production.

Ellie Collyer-Bristow – Casting Director

Recent credits include: *Dusty* (UK tour); *Monogamy* (UK tour and Park Theatre); *Turn of the Screw* (Mercury Theatre and UK tour); *Witness for the Prosecution* (County Hall, Southbank); children's casting for *The King and I* (London Palladium); *Jack and the Beanstalk* (Salisbury Playhouse); *Cookies* (Theatre Royal Haymarket); *Wait Until Dark* (UK tour); *Wordsworth, Two Way Mirror, After the Dance, As You Like It, Handbagged, Remarkable Invisible, Miss Julie and The Secret Garden* (Theatre by the Lake); *A Lie of the Mind and Doubt, a Parable* (Southwark Playhouse); *Madame Rubinstein* (Park Theatre); *Dirty Great Love Story* (Arts Theatre); *Fool for Love* (Found 111); children's casting for *The Wind in the Willows* (London Palladium); *Much Ado About Nothing* (reFASHIONed Theatre @ Selfridges for the Faction); *French Without Tears* (Orange Tree/ETT – UK tour); *Night Must Fall* (Salisbury Playhouse/Original Theatre Company – UK tour); *Sideways* (St James Theatre); *Gaslight* (Ed Mirvish, Toronto); *The Glass Menagerie* (Nuffield, Southampton); *Dancing at*

Lughnasa (Lyric Theatre, Belfast); *Handbagged* (Eleanor Lloyd Productions – UK tour); *The Gathered Leaves* (Park Theatre); *Arcadia* (ETT – UK tour); *Told Look Younger* (Jermyn Street); *Eldorado* (Arcola); *Tape* (Trafalgar Studios); *Blue Remembered Hills*, *Playhouse Creatures* and *Fred's Diner* (Chichester Festival Theatre); *Four Nights in Knaresborough* (Southwark Playhouse); *Fings Ain't Wot They Used t'Be* and *Bernarda Alba (Union) and This Is How It Goes* and *A Christmas Carol* (King's Head). Ellie was previously casting associate for the Ambassador Theatre Group.

ADDITIONAL PROGRAMME CREDITS

Scenic Painters: Sidra Hussain Laura Fessey

Costume Assistants: Eleanor Robberts
Collette Robinson-Collcutt

Special Thanks to: Herne Hill Harriers

Sarah Rutherford

THE GIRL WHO FELL

OBERON BOOKS
LONDON

WWW.OBERONBOOKS.COM

First published in 2019 by Oberon Books Ltd
521 Caledonian Road, London N7 9RH
Tel: +44 (0) 20 7607 3637 / Fax: +44 (0) 20 7607 3629
e-mail: info@oberonbooks.com
www.oberonbooks.com

PB ISBN: 9781786829672
E ISBN: 9781786829689

Cover image: feastcreative.com

10 9 8 7 6 5 4 3 2 1

To my parents,
Ros and Alan Rutherford

'Living is keeping the absurd alive.'

Albert Camus, *The Myth of Sisyphus*

Acknowledgements

I am indebted to the following for their support and involvement with the play in development: Jassa Ahluwalia, Rakie Ayola, Donna Banya, Roly Botha, Hadley Fraser, Lucy Heath, Louise McNamara, Nicholas Pinnock, Charlotte Randle, Ria Zmitrowicz and all at Park Theatre.

I am also grateful to my agent Emily Hickman; to Gemma Birt, Dr Robin Hadley and Susanne Sivagnanam for their help with research; to Nina Madden for getting me unstuck; and to the Arvon Foundation for all the peace.

And endless thanks to Danny, Ruby and Carmen for all the encouragement, inspiration, laughs and love.

SCENE ONE

LENNY (15) bounds into the park, closely followed by his significantly smaller twin, BILLIE, who propels herself along on a single rollerskate.

They're both in black outfits.

LENNY's is a pseudo-gangsta-style ensemble with a saxophone incongruously slung on a strap over his shoulder.

BILLIE wears sparkly silver shoes, a rollerskate strapped to one of them.

LENNY: It's like being eaten up from the inside.

BILLIE: *(Still going – circling and spinning.)* It's not *like* being eaten up from the inside. It *is* being eaten up from the inside. By your *friends.* Go on, play.

LENNY: I'm not playing.

BILLIE: Shut up.

LENNY: What do you mean, eaten by your friends?

BILLIE: Friendly bacteria. Gut flora. When you're alive, you'd be lost without them. Hence the marketability of the probiotic yogurt drink. Play your fucking sax or I'm going home.

LENNY: So when you're dead

BILLIE: That's why they don't seal coffins any more.

LENNY: What, why?

BILLIE: Think about it. What are the by-products of the digestive process?

LENNY: I dunno. Gas…es?

BILLIE: Methane. As in

LENNY makes a spectacular farting noise.

Exactly. There have been cases of extreme post-mortem bloating, leading to…

LENNY: No.

BILLIE: Exploded right out of the final resting place.

LENNY: And people chat about worms.

BILLIE: 'We fat all creatures else to fat us, and we fat ourselves for maggots.' That's Shakespeare. More likely you'll burst if your body's intact to start with, though.

LENNY gives this some thought.

LENNY: When I die, yeah? Crush me flat.

BILLIE: Wicked Witch of the East style.

LENNY: Use one of them junkyard car crusher things.

BILLIE: With great pleasure.

LENNY: And if you die first?

BILLIE: I won't. Why did you bring your sax if you're not going to play it?

LENNY: Selling it.

BILLIE: What, today?

LENNY: Said I'd meet JD later and show it him.

BILLIE: JD doesn't play sax.

LENNY: No but there's this fit girl in concert band, so. Unless you want to learn? Do you a good deal? Friends and family?

BILLIE: Mum wouldn't let you sell it to me, it was Uncle Derek's. Anyway, you're the musician. So you say.

LENNY: Not my style any more.

BILLIE: Here we go. Not fooling anybody with your fucking makeover you know.

LENNY: It's called growing up.

BILLIE: You were shit at jazz anyway. This is your way of saving face.

LENNY: What, like when you gave up singing after I got Grade 1 Distinction and you got Merit?

BILLIE: How do you even remember that? We were like seven.

LENNY: Don't pretend / you don't remember

BILLIE: Most people die on the shitter you know.

LENNY: No they don't.

BILLIE: All right. Most people die in bed. But after that, the most common place is on the double-you-cee. You going to ask me why?

LENNY: No.

BILLIE: Because, if you have like a massive heart attack, or you've got a clot on your lung, which are common terminal events, what it feels like is that you need to do a humungous pile of faeces.

LENNY: So you rush to the bog and you go *(he mimes straining and then dying)*. Brilliant.

BILLIE: That's how you'll go.

LENNY: And it'll be you that finds me. D'you think they did a post-mortem?

BILLIE: Definitely. Sudden and violent death. Want to know about that too?

LENNY: No.

3

Yes.

BILLIE: Well they start with an incision from the sternum to the pubic / bone

LENNY: Would we have been allowed to see her?

BILLIE: … We saw her.

LENNY: No, I mean like in the funeral home. Did they have like a viewing?

BILLIE: Did you want to press your mouth to her lily lips, her cherry nose, her yellow cowslip cheeks, her eyes as green as leeks?

LENNY: She didn't have green eyes. I don't think.

BILLIE: I've got this:

She produces a length of red hair tied with a ribbon.

LENNY: *Fuuuuuuuck!* What the fuck is that?

BILLIE: She brought it to school. Think she thought maybe I could stick it back on for her or something.

LENNY: She wasn't stupid.

BILLIE: Didn't say she was stupid! I know she wasn't stupid, I knew her better than anyone.

LENNY: *Really.*

BILLIE: Tried to plait it – there was this long bit hanging, did you see? I tried to weave this bit in with that, to make it look like a plait. Didn't work. Here.

LENNY: I'm not touching it!

BILLIE: And you reckon you'd've fancied seeing her corpse without *swooning*?

LENNY: I'm not scared, I'm just –

BILLIE: Smell it.

LENNY: Fuck off.

BILLIE: Pussy.

He sniffs the hair. BILLIE strokes his face with it.

Ooh Lenny! Bring back memories? You can have it if you like. Wrap it round your little weenie when you think about her.

LENNY: If you was her friend you'd have more respect.

BILLIE: If you were her boyfriend, you'd play her some music. Cancel out that shitty funeral that never even mentioned how she died. Give her a proper send-off. Ease her on down the road. I mean look! *(She points to her shoes.)* This is her day! Munchkins! Flying biker monkeys! Michael Jackson and Diana Ross! You're shit.

LENNY: I bought these.

He pulls out a packet of seeds.

BILLIE: Fuck's that?

He shows her.

LENNY: … Poppies. You know: sssssssssssss…

BILLIE: The deadly prostitutes.

LENNY: They're not prostitutes, they're flowers.

BILLIE: They're poisonous slags that throw fucking drugs in your face and then you end up unconscious in a big pink / tunnel

LENNY: It's a packet of seeds, Bill.

BILLIE: What are you going to do with them?

LENNY: Sow them?

BILLIE: Here?

LENNY: Oh look, I'm going to go and meet JD, / get rid of this

BILLIE: Go on then. If that's all you've got. You've got to do something for her today.

LENNY: This is so lame.

He reads the instructions. BILLIE snatches the packet from him, scatters the seeds around the bench.

There's more to it than that!

BILLIE: In World War One, they sprang out of nowhere, didn't they? 'We are the Dead. Short days ago we lived, felt dawn, saw sunset glow, *luuuurved* and were / *luuuuurved*'

LENNY: Oh shut up with your fucking Shakespeare.

BILLIE: Yeah 'cos Shakespeare was totally alive in the First World War.

LENNY: Might be a different kind of poppy! And that was my thing!

BILLIE: Won't grow anyway. How many flowers have you seen around here? Bet the soil's toxic or something.

LENNY: We should put one of them metal things on the bench.

BILLIE: A plaque? You'd definitely need permission for that.

LENNY: Plaque. Aren't they just for famous people?

BILLIE: She is famous now.

LENNY: So what did you bring?

BILLIE pulls out a single, green, uninflated balloon.

BILLIE: *And* the shoes. D'you think anybody got that? Apart from her mum maybe.

LENNY: Her mum? Does she even know about Sam and *The Wiz*?

BILLIE: Everybody knew about Sam and *The Wiz*.

LENNY: Her mum didn't know the first thing about her! If she had, she wouldn't have done what she did!

BILLIE: I couldn't stand being in the same room as her, to be honest. All those people hugging her and stuff like she didn't kill her own daughter.

LENNY: So what's the green condom for? Booty call with Shrek?

BILLIE: The Wizard. Herman Smith, the balloonist from Atlantic City.

If I had a full-size air balloon I'd've brought that, obviously.

LENNY: You got that from our old birthday box in the loft.

BILLIE: So?

LENNY: I went Sainsbury's for this!

BILLIE: Not a competition.

LENNY: Riiight… So what's your grand gesture?

BILLIE: I was going to – you know – I mean now that I'm saying it I realise I need a helium canister –

LENNY: Just blow it up.

She blows it up.

Good lungs.

BILLIE: What do I do now? Tie a knot?

LENNY: Let it go. That's the plan, isn't it?

BILLIE: But it's not going to float.

LENNY: Just let it go, it'll be fine.

BILLIE: … Sam, this is for you.

> *BILLIE pauses dramatically, lets it go and it zips around them, making a farting noise. LENNY laughs uncontrollably.*

Fuck you! Fuck you, that was my tribute to my best fucking friend! I hate you!

> *LENNY bolts, pursued by BILLIE.*

SCENE TWO

THEA's house – extreme order and organisation overlaid with a few days' chaos and squalor.

THEA (40s), dishevelled and unwashed, sits contemplating a row of pill bottles and a litre of whisky.

Just as she lifts the whisky bottle, the doorbell rings.

At first she covers her ears, but as the ringing gets more insistent she gives up, sweeps the bottles into a bin bag, pulls herself together as much as she can, and opens the door a crack.

It's BILLIE, in school uniform (and one skate).

BILLIE: Hi.

THEA: Hi Billie.

BILLIE: Mum told me to bring you this.

> *Tries to squeeze a tub through the crack in the door.*

Um… You're going to have to open the door a bit.

THEA opens the door just enough to let the tub through.

THEA: Thanks.

BILLIE: … Mum said I had to come in and make you a cup
of tea.

THEA: What? No, you don't have to do that.

BILLIE: She says I do. She went on about it.

It's a stand-off.

THEA: Right. OK. Come in then. It's a bit of a mess I'm
afraid.

She lets BILLIE in.

BILLIE: That's all right, Mum warned me it would be a bit of
a pigsty.

*THEA puts the tub on top of a pile of identical tubs, all still full of
food. BILLIE unstraps her rollerskate.*

It's not homemade, that one.

THEA: That's OK.

BILLIE: She'd've come herself but Dad said she needed a
night off from you.

They're nice though, those ones. If I hadn't told you,
you'd never have known.

THEA: She's a good friend.

BILLIE: Must be nice to have someone who's known you
practically all your life.

THEA: You've got a *twin*.

BILLIE: … Yeah – but Lenny's Lenny.

THEA: Where is he?

BILLIE: Home. Watching porn probably.

THEA: Right.

BILLIE: Oh and that's rocket.

THEA: Oh. Great.

BILLIE: Really?

THEA: Yeah. I like rocket.

BILLIE looks at her like she's an alien.

Do you want a juice or something?

BILLIE: Fruit juice has about the same amount of sugar as Coke. Shall I make you a cup of tea?

THEA: You can dilute it.

BILLIE: Tea?

THEA: Juice. I'll do it, it's fine. Do you want one?

BILLIE: Only drink White Chocolate Mochas.

THEA: How's school?

BILLIE: It's all right. They're doing all these special assemblies and on-demand counselling.

THEA: Oh. Good.

BILLIE: Children are widely considered to be remarkably resilient.

THEA: Yeah. Some are, yeah. Did you like the funeral?

BILLIE: No. Sorry.

THEA: It's all right.

BILLIE: Did you like it?

THEA: No.

BILLIE: Why didn't you do it yourself? Thought you were a vicar.

THEA: I'm a chaplain, it's a bit different. And I wouldn't have wanted to anyway.

BILLIE: Was that her dad that was there?

THEA: Yeah.

BILLIE: Mum said it was nice he turned up when it mattered.

THEA: … Yeah.

I liked your shoes.

BILLIE: Oh, thanks.

They look at each other for a moment. THEA is barely holding it together.

BILLIE: Well if you don't want me to do the tea –

THEA: Can you take these back to your mum?

THEA gathers up a pile of self-help books.

BILLIE: I thought you liked books.

THEA: Tell her they were… just tell her thanks.

BILLIE: But they're all written for / exactly

THEA: Yes I know, but Billie – look, I know you're young but you're an intelligent girl –

BILLIE: No I'm not.

THEA: Open any of those books at random. Go on, read a page, any page.

BILLIE: All right. 'Guilt.'

THEA: Ha!

BILLIE: What?

THEA: Carry on.

BILLIE: 'At some stage of the grieving process, guilt is inevitable. But guilt after suicide is a false accusation.'

THEA: See? False accusation! Go on.

BILLIE: 'We cannot predict the actions of others, / and we cannot' –

THEA: Crap! Not the point! We can predict our *own* actions. It's all bollocks.

She grabs the book.

'Nothing you could have done would have prevented their death.' That's shit! Something I *did* do *caused* her death! It's back to front! None of this has anything to do with me! It's for people who are racking their brains for something like, maybe they didn't say they loved them the last time they talked, or… This is not for people like me!

BILLIE: … Are vicars supposed to swear?

THEA: I'm not a fucking vicar!

Sorry.

Do you think she meant to do it?

BILLIE: What?

THEA: There's no note. There's no one else I can ask.

I mean I know you don't accidentally fall off a bridge like that, I know she –

But did she plan it, did she…?

BILLIE: I think… I think she was really sad.

THEA: Yeah.

Because of what I did.

BILLIE: … Yeah.

THEA: And where is she now, do you think?

BILLIE: Where is she? You mean her body, / or

THEA: Where is *she?* What's she doing, what's she seeing, who's, you know, who's looking after her now?

BILLIE: You're the… whatsit.

THEA: I know. I'm supposed to have all the answers. And normally I do. But the fact is, she's gone somewhere I… I've never been there – I've never seen it – what do I know?

BILLIE: The undiscovered country.

THEA: … You know Shakespeare.

BILLIE: No.

THEA: She didn't ask if she could go, Billie, she just went. And she knows things now, things I should've been able to help her with or advise her on, and she can't even – you know how I used to make her text 'On bus', 'Off bus'? It's like – there should be someone I can complain to, it's not acceptable, she's too young…

BILLIE: Isn't she in Heaven though?

THEA: 'In reality there is no experience of death. It is barely possible to speak of the experience of others' deaths. It is a substitute, an illusion, and it never quite convinces us.'

BILLIE: Don't think that's Shakespeare.

THEA: You're right. Camus.

BILLIE: Who?

THEA: Footballer.

BILLIE: You don't want to listen to footballers.

THEA: Well, he wasn't just a footballer.

THEA hands BILLIE a well-thumbed copy of The Myth of Sisyphus.

BILLIE: I don't really read books.

THEA: What about *Hamlet*?

BILLIE: That's the only bit I know. Oh and the maggots. And 'Is she to be buried in Christian burial?'

THEA: Not 'To be or not to be?'

BILLIE: It's just an app. New quote every day. You can get random ones or you can choose the subject. Useful facts as well, I like facts. I'm on it all the time since I gave up social media.

THEA: Oh? When did you do that?

BILLIE: When all the stink started about Sam. It's *so hard*, giving it up. My friends would find it a lot more normal if I'd gone to Syria and joined ISIS or something.

THEA: But the video got taken down?

BILLIE: You can't really take things like that down. Somebody videoed the video, talk about low-tech. So every time it gets deleted, it pops up somewhere else.

THEA: I should look, shouldn't I.

BILLIE: I wouldn't. There's some nutters out there, / and you're

THEA: Can't they find out who these people are? Or who posted it in the first place? The police are still on my back – shouldn't they be chasing them?

BILLIE: Don't think they can really. It's all over the world.

THEA: The *world*?

BILLIE: Well. Probably just the English-speaking world, I don't know.

Think I should go now, check on Lenny.

THEA: 'Course. Thanks for coming.

BILLIE: I didn't really have a choice.

THEA: No. Thanks for the pie though.

BILLIE: And the rocket.

THEA: And the rocket.

SCENE THREE

A neighbourhood ice cream parlour. THEA is hunched over a vast, elaborate sundae – spoon in one hand, book in the other.

GIL (40s, smart) enters, pocketing his change, steaming coffee in hand. He looks at THEA for a moment.

GIL: Defeated?

She looks up with a start. He indicates the sundae.

Bit of a challenge, that.

She looks from the book to the ice cream and back again.

The sundae.

Feel out of place with just this.

He takes a sip, burns his tongue.

You're waiting for someone.

Two spoons.

THEA: No, I'm…

No.

She looks down, eats. He doesn't go away.

Are you waiting for me to justify the size of my ice cream, or

GIL: No! God no. None of my business. Although it is *huge!*
No. I'm kidding.

Any chance I could sit down for a second? People are
staring at me like I'm chatting you up or something.
(He sits.) Just to drink this. I won't interrupt your reading.

THEA closes her book.

THEA: It's all right, it's not very good.

GIL picks it up.

GIL: Holy Bible? Is that to atone / for

THEA: You've got a real problem with me eating this, haven't
you?

GIL: No! Really. You just don't look like the kind of person
who –

THEA hands him the other spoon.

No it's fine, I wasn't –

Well. Thanks. *(He eats.)* Jesus fucking Christ this is good.
Sorry.

They eat in silence for a moment.

So. Zero stars on Amazon for the Holy Bible.

THEA: Ever read it?

GIL: Bits. When I was a kid. Fancied myself as a proper
Christian for a few years. Used to read that – not your
fancy one, some modernised easy-reader version. Even
memorised whole chunks. Till I discovered a few things I
reckoned God probably didn't endorse.

THEA: Still believe any of it?

GIL: Some days I do. Fair-weather Christian.

THEA: You pray?

GIL: When I need to. I'm like one of those brats who only
rings his grandma when he's short of cash. I prayed just
recently now I think about it.

THEA: And you believe in Heaven and Hell?

GIL: Um, yeah. No. Not... Some kind of afterlife. I guess. I
hope.

THEA: Wow.

GIL: You don't?

THEA: ... Isn't it a bit... ungrateful?

GIL: Ungrateful?

THEA: Like one life isn't enough. It's a cop-out, isn't it? Gives
people an excuse not to really live. As long as they more
or less stay out of trouble, they'll get a harp and a pair of
sandals on the other side. Or a bunch of virgins, or I don't
know, mead and Valkyries, or –

Sorry. I don't really do small talk.

GIL: Oh I do. So: is this a regular treat?

THEA: Yeah – breakfast, lunch and dinner.

GIL: No, I wasn't –

THEA: You were asking if I come here often.

GIL: Something like that.

THEA: Once a week or so.

Once a week. Exactly.

GIL: It's nice. Pricey, but

THEA: Not for artisanal gelato. It's a bargain.

GIL: If you say so. So is this your lunchbreak, or

THEA: Um no. I'm not working at the moment.

GIL: Lady of leisure. So what do you do when you are working?

THEA: Nothing interesting.

GIL: Go on.

THEA: I've just been… helping out in the prison. You?

GIL: I help out in a theatre.

THEA: Sounds glamorous.

GIL: Operating theatre.

THEA: Oh.

GIL: Consultant anaesthetist.

THEA: You put people to sleep.

GIL: I ease their pain.

THEA: You never hear about gentlemen of leisure, do you?

GIL: Doesn't alliterate. Doesn't sound very respectable, either.

THEA: Doesn't it?

GIL: Sounds like a euphemism for some kind of high-class gigolo. Or is that just me.

THEA: I don't know, is it?

GIL: No, I mean

THEA: It would explain you accosting lonely middle-aged women in expensive establishments.

GIL: What middle-aged women?

THEA: So you admit to the accosting bit?

GIL: And you admit to the lonely bit?

Sorry, that was… I was just teasing.

THEA: It's fine.

GIL: No, I've messed up now.

THEA: Messed what up?

GIL: No, I was just thinking maybe I would ask for your number.

THEA freezes.

I know, that took me by surprise too. Only popped in here 'cos the coffee looked good. Which it is by the way. Artisanal.

Anyway, I've enjoyed talking to you. It's been… intense. And I'm sure you're married, to a really good guy who doesn't judge what you're eating and who definitely doesn't call you a 'lady of leisure' when you're taking some well-earned time out. Right?

THEA: Well no, actually. About the married bit. Was once, but… not even to a good guy.

GIL: So… Maybe I give you *my* number? And you can chuck it in one of those vintage shabby-chic bins when my back's turned. Anyway.

He starts writing on a napkin.

THEA: I'm… I'm going to say no.

GIL: … Right. No, of course, that's fine. I've been really… intrusive.

THEA: I just… wouldn't want to take it and then not call. I hate that kind of… Better just to say, now.

GIL: OK. Well –

THEA: I've enjoyed talking to you too. It's been… the opposite of intense.

GIL: … Fun?

THEA: I – yeah. Like a sort of –

GIL: Escape?

THEA: – bubble. Or something.

GIL: Right. But not a bubble that you'd like to… revisit.

SCENE FOUR

THEA's house. Worse than before.

An extremely clumsily-iced green birthday cake sits on the table with 16 candles burning down, watched by THEA, who's well into the bottle of whisky – but no pills this time.

Doorbell.

THEA: *(Under her breath.)* Oh fuck off.

Doorbell keeps ringing. Eventually THEA gives in.

It's LENNY.

Oh Lenny, I've got so much food, I'm really honestly fine.

LENNY: I haven't brought food… I brought a present for Sam.

THEA: A present…

LENNY: Bought it ages ago. Getting a bit sick of looking at it if I'm honest. Thought you might know what to do with it.

THEA: You'd better come in.

LENNY enters, sees the cake.

LENNY: Oh.

THEA: Did it myself.

LENNY: Nice.

They contemplate it.

THEA: Do you want to blow out the candles?

LENNY: Nah, you're all right.

THEA: Go on. Makes more sense than me doing it.

LENNY: It's OK. I'll just leave this, and maybe you can… put it in her room or something.

THEA: Could you blow out the candles, please?

LENNY: … All right.

He does so, while THEA pours an extra glass of whisky. She hands it to him.

THEA: Here.

LENNY: What's this?

THEA: Try it, it's nice.

LENNY sips. Hides a wince.

LENNY: Yeah, it's good.

THEA: Can I open it?

LENNY: Oh, I was just going to – OK –

It's a necklace with a green stone.

It's not a real emerald, / but

THEA: Nice though. You were a good boyfriend.

LENNY: Thanks.

THEA: It was a bit weird at first, for me, but… better the devil you know or something.

LENNY: Yeah.

THEA: Shall we cut it?

LENNY: What? Oh. Nah, it's OK. I just wanted to drop this off.

THEA: I won't tell anyone.

LENNY: What?

THEA: That you came over. It's all right, I know what people think of me.

She hands him a big knife. He's thrown for a moment.

You can scream when it hits the plate if you like.

LENNY: Why did you and Sam always do that?

THEA: It's a thing. I always used to think it was all the little crumbs crying out in pain. Go on.

LENNY: I'm all right thanks.

THEA: No go on. When it hits the plate. Scream. Go on.

LENNY lets out a bloodcurdling scream.

THEA: Jesus.   LENNY: Sorry.

THEA: Shall we do a toast?

LENNY: Um…

THEA: Something about Sam, come on.

LENNY: Um… I wish she was here…

THEA: Yeah… Anything else?

LENNY: She was… really… *I don't know…* I liked her. A lot.

THEA: OK… Well… I just want to say…

She pauses. Shuts her eyes. LENNY looks confused, then shuts his eyes too and clasps his hands as if in prayer.

Sam: happy birthday… I hope you're celebrating wherever you are, I hope someone's made you a better cake than this one, and if you get the chance, send us a… message. Some kind of sign.

LENNY looks alarmed at this idea.

And um, yeah. I'm sorry. I know you hated all my quotes, but Charlotte Brontë said remorse is the poison of life. And it is. So. I hope your… death… is better than my life.

… Lenny.

LENNY starts and opens his eyes.

LENNY: Sorry.

THEA: So. That's that. How's your mum?

LENNY: What? Oh, she's OK.

THEA: Haven't seen her for a while.

LENNY: Oh.

THEA: It's OK.

How's the music?

LENNY: Oh. I gave up the sax.

THEA: No! First Billie with the singing, / and now

LENNY: I'm into other stuff now. Writing my own stuff, mixing…

THEA: Oh. Well. That sounds creative. Is that what the change of image is for?

LENNY: No.

She gives him a huge slab of cake. He tastes it and then puts it back down.

THEA: Still running?

LENNY: Yeah. More than ever. Training like crazy.

THEA: As long as you don't overdo it.

LENNY: Nah, I'm good.

THEA: You ever fainted?

LENNY: What, when I'm training?

THEA: I saw someone faint in the prison gym once, got a bit overheated I think. Big tattooed bloke swooning like some Victorian heroine. Looked dead. Never happened to you?

LENNY: No. Well, not like that.

THEA: Like what then?

LENNY: We did it on purpose once. Year 6. Probably not that clever.

THEA: What was it like?

LENNY: Um, weird. Kind of trippy.

THEA: Tunnel of light and all that?

LENNY: Yeah. It was nice, now I think of it. Peaceful. Like sort of floating into this other world. But then I came to and vomited down my school jumper.

THEA: How did you do it?

LENNY: Oh, I don't remember.

THEA: Yes you do.

She pours him another whisky.

More cake?

LENNY: I'm good thanks. It's got a name, we looked it up: Vancouver something.

THEA: Valsalva manoeuvre.

LENNY: That's right.

THEA: Did Sam do it?

LENNY: Um… not sure. We was just friends then.

THEA: Show me.

LENNY: What?

THEA: Show me what you did.

LENNY: What, now?

THEA: I'm interested.

LENNY: Nah, I don't…

THEA: Go on, it'll be fun. You're allowed to have fun, you
know. Do us both good. I'll do it with you.

LENNY: You sure?

THEA: Yeah! Go on.

LENNY looks at her, takes a big gulp of whisky.

LENNY: Well you squat down, and you breathe in and out
really fast…

THEA copies him. He splutters a bit.

THEA: Go on.

LENNY: OK, well you do that for a while, and then you
breathe against your arm for a bit.

Bit longer…

And then you stand up suddenly.

*They both stand up quickly, and LENNY immediately faints. THEA
looks down at him.*

THEA: Oh shit.

SCENE FIVE

THEA's doorstep. THEA opens the door. Stops. Goes back inside. Returns with a dustpan and brush. Starts brushing here and there at first, then with more and more ferocity and desperation.

GIL appears.

GIL: Hey! It *is* you. You OK?

> *THEA stops, looks at him.*

From the ice cream place. Food police? We talked about God, you crushed my ego?

THEA: … Why are you here?

GIL: I was going to get another one of those artisanal coffees before work. Guess it's your local, that place. Sorry, is it a bit – I mean it's just there, I was –

THEA: No, it's… You're on a public… pavement.

GIL: Sorry if I embarrassed you that day.

THEA: I'm not that easily embarrassed.

GIL: Well. Harassed you then. I don't normally do that, it was… really… crass.

THEA: It was… just bad timing.

GIL: OK. Well. I apologise for my extremely poor timing.

THEA: … How are you.

GIL: Good thanks. Busy. I mean, that's a relative term for an anaesthetist. Hours of boredom, minutes of thrill, seconds of terror. You still off work?

THEA: For now.

GIL: Well, enjoy it.

THEA leans back against the doorframe.

You all right?

THEA: Yeah I'm fine, it's just… I'm fine.

She starts to retch.

GIL: Oh God, um –

THEA: *(Feeling for her keys.)* Honestly I'm fine, I'll just go back inside, I'll be OK –

GIL: Sit down a second. Can you sit down? Just take a few deep breaths.

THEA: It's just – it's all this… shit, I can't seem to

GIL: All this what?

THEA: It's disgusting, it disgusts me, can't you see

GIL: Would you let me go in, get you some water?

No, sorry. It's OK, look –

He gives her a bottle of water from his bag.

It's OK it's OK. Do you need to be sick? All right. All right.

THEA: Someone leaves it here. Dumps it here.

GIL: Dumps what?

THEA: Hair. Human hair. Every morning I open the door and there's this big pile of… clippings or something, all different colours, all blowing around on my doorstep and every morning I clean it up and it gets all over me, it mixes in with *my* hair, it gets in my mouth, I can't

GIL: I don't see anything.

THEA: That's because I cleaned it all up, but even when it's gone it blows back and it's everywhere, and now every strand of hair, every single hair I see

She retches again.

GIL: You need to go inside, sit down, take it easy. Is there someone inside I can call for you?

I mean I can't just… Let me phone someone for you.

THEA: I'm fine.

GIL: Well no, you're obviously not, so

THEA: What's it to you anyway?

GIL: My mum always taught me not to pass by on the other side of the street.

THEA: The Bible again.

GIL: Oh. You do remember our chat, at least.

I promise I'm not an axe-murderer, this is on my route to work. Look *(his business card)*, that's my mobile number. OK? Purely for emergency purposes this time.

THEA: Really, you / don't need to

GIL: Just in case. Please. I'll feel better if you take it.

And from nowhere there's a whoop of joy.

SCENE SIX

Race track. LENNY bursts in, whooping and performing an infectious and acrobatic victory dance.

BILLIE scrolls through her phone, unimpressed.

LENNY: I won – I won – I'm the best – I'm the best –

He runs towards her, arms outstretched. She scoots away.

BILLIE: Get off! You're all slimy!

LENNY: Healthy man-sweat. Top-quality pheromones.

BILLIE: Can we go now?

LENNY: Were you even watching?

BILLIE: Mum said I had to video it if she didn't make it on time. She never said I had to dress up as a cheerleader and sing a little song.

LENNY: No one would want to see *that*.

Come on then, what's your top quote about winners?

BILLIE taps her phone. Declaims.

BILLIE: 'these punks
these cowards
these champions
these mad dogs of glory
moving this little bit of light toward
us
impossibly'

LENNY: … What?

BILLIE: Some of these, you have to think about. They're not just, like, 'He who runs fast gets a fucking sticker.'

LENNY: It's a medal.

BILLIE: Whatever. It's from a poem, anyway. In a *book*. Called *You Get So Alone at Times That it Just Makes Sense*.

LENNY: Nothing you say makes any sense.

BILLIE: Not to you, 'cos you're such a child.

LENNY: Yeah. Obvious thing to insult your twin about. His *age*.

BILLIE: The only people who think you're the older one are people who haven't heard you speak.

LENNY: Know what, Bill? I could be just as rude, but I wouldn't want you to think I was, you know, *looking down* on you.

BILLIE: Why are we still here, anyway?

LENNY: Bill. I *won*. I'm in the final.

BILLIE: What? I'm freezing my tits off here!

LENNY: What tits?

BILLIE: Fuck *off!* Just 'cos Sam never showed you hers.

LENNY: Says who?

BILLIE: I mean apart from in the photos she posted. But then the whole world got to see them. Not the same, is it?

LENNY: Shut up about Sam. You don't know anything.

BILLIE: About my best friend.

LENNY: Says you.

BILLIE: Least I still think about her. Here you are, mincing about in your little shorts like she never existed.

LENNY: How does not running help Sam in any way?

BILLIE: And you chucked her birthday present in the bin.

LENNY: What? No I didn't.

BILLIE: Where is it then?

LENNY: None of your business.

BILLIE: Did you take it back to the shop?

LENNY: No.

BILLIE: Yes you did. 'Can I have my pocket money back? My girlfriend smashed herself to bits on somebody's car roof so I don't need this any more.'

LENNY: I didn't take it back!

BILLIE: I know it's not in your room any more. Did you give it to someone else?

LENNY: No!

BILLIE: Who is it? She must be pretty dumb if she doesn't know it was for Sam.

LENNY: It was Sam's mum, all right?

BILLIE: You gave a necklace to Sam's mum?

LENNY: Not like that! Fuck's sake, Bill.

BILLIE: Suppose she's quite fit now she's stopped wearing that dog collar. Or is that what turns you on?

LENNY: Bill. She barely washes these days. And she *killed Sam*. We agreed on that. The police'll charge her any day now. Sam was happy till her mum went mental.

BILLIE: How would you know how happy she was?

LENNY: I knew how to make her happy.

BILLIE: Listen to yourself. You didn't know anything about what was going on in her head. She just liked the abstract idea of having a boyfriend, and you were the safe option.

LENNY: Safe?

BILLIE: Friend of the family, nice and familiar, not too – you know – alpha.

LENNY: I'm alpha. I am. I am fucking alpha. What do you mean by alpha?

BILLIE: Oh my God.

LENNY: If you knew her so well, you tell me what was going on in her head. You can't, can you?

A loudhailer announcement. LENNY turns to go.

You've got no idea. All you could do was fuck about with ponytails. If you were her friend, why didn't she talk to you? Why didn't she tell you what she was going to do? Why didn't she pour out her heart the way girls are supposed to do? You weren't her friend, you was just a hanger-on. You're the designated ugly friend. Every fit girl has one.

BILLIE: Oh, go back to your neanderthal running races, *Leonard.* I know a *lot.*

LENNY: Oh stop saying that! If you really knew a lot, you'd tell me. I know you, you can't help airing your knowledge. Trust me, you know jack shit.

BILLIE: You're wrong. Can't say any more but you're wrong. She confided in me. *Leaned* on me.

LENNY: Why don't you just start running again? You were quite good once.

BILLIE: *Quite* good? What's that got to do with anything?

LENNY: You gave up when I started winning. Same with everything.

BILLIE: I gave up when I realised it was for shit-for-brains primitives. So you can run faster than the next person, so what? What does that achieve? What does it prove? Where does it get you in life? I mean it's quite symbolic, isn't it, the way you run round that track and arrive back where you started. In what situation would you ever be required to run five kilometres? Isn't that what cars are for? It's meaningless, Lenny. It's a distraction. It's like God and Snapchat – anything to stop people *thinking* and questioning things.

LENNY: I am questioning things! I'm questioning you, and you're not answering! Because we all know Thea killed Sam, but you have to go and build it up into some kind of big mystery that only you know the answer to. Stop trying to get attention, *Wilma*, it's pathetic.

BILLIE: She gave me her phone.

LENNY: … She what?

BILLIE: Day she died. Gave me her phone, asked me to look after it.

LENNY: This gets sadder by the minute. She had her phone on her when she died. That basic dumb-phone her mum made her use. It's in all the reports.

BILLIE: She had another phone.

LENNY: No she didn't. She'd've told me.

BILLIE: You know the Samsung that got confiscated? She found it, stuck in some old shoebox at the back of her mum's wardrobe. How'd you think she was posting so much?

LENNY: … So what's on the phone?

BILLIE: Haven't looked at everything on it. She told me to look at the notes.

LENNY: And?

BILLIE: Nothing to do with you. No love letters or anything, don't get your hopes up.

LENNY: What then? I've got to go and run in a second.

BILLIE: Go on then, nobody's stopping you. It's nothing anyway.

LENNY: Must be something if you're making such a big fucking deal out of it.

BILLIE: Just pointing out, it was me she gave it to. That's all. She trusted me. I was her friend. Now run off and do your skipping race, or is it the egg-and-spoon next?

A whistle sounds. LENNY waves, then grabs BILLIE.

LENNY: Quick. Tell me what's on that phone.

BILLIE: Oh is this you trying to be alpha now?

LENNY: Tell me!

BILLIE: Ow! A note to her mum, that's all.

LENNY: What, like a suicide note? You'd better be kidding. What if the police find it?

BILLIE: I'm not on trial. And they still haven't charged her mum with anything either, which is a crime in itself.

LENNY: But this is withholding evidence or something! What does it say?

BILLIE: Pretty standard.

The whistle again.

LENNY: But *what?*

BILLIE: That she's sorry, that it's not her mum's fault, that it's nothing to do with what she did. Not to be sad. That she loves her. That kind of crap. Doesn't explain anything.

LENNY: Except that she didn't blame her mum. *Billie.*

Whistle. Shouts. LENNY turns to go.

You're an idiot, Bill.

BILLIE: Fuck off.

SCENE SEVEN

THEA's house. THEA enters with GIL, laughing.

GIL: There's poetry in it, too.

THEA: 'And the haft also went in after the blade; and the fat closed upon the blade, so that he could not draw the dagger out of his belly; and the dirt came out.'

GIL: That's not the Bible, that's a horror film.

THEA: Judges 3, verse 22.

GIL: You'd been reading for longer than I thought that day! What about the Psalms?

THEA: What *about* the Psalms?

GIL: You didn't read them?

THEA: Go on, tell me about the Psalms.

GIL: Listen.
   'For my days vanish like smoke;
   my bones burn like glowing embers.
   My heart is blighted and withered like grass;
   I forget to eat my food.
   In my distress I groan aloud
   and am reduced to skin and bones.
   I am like a desert owl,
   like an owl among the ruins.
   I lie awake; I have become
   like a bird alone on a roof.
   All day long my enemies taunt me;
   those who rail against me use my name as a curse.

For I eat ashes as my food
and mingle my drink with tears.'

THEA is floored and struggles to hide it.

THEA: … Why pick that one?

GIL: Told you, I used to commit whole chunks to memory. I liked the depressing bits. Sorry, that was a bit of a downer. I like your house.

THEA: … I should probably clean it more. You want something to eat?

GIL: God no, I'm full of ice cream.

THEA: You hardly touched it.

GIL: I've learned not to get between you and your dessert.

THEA: More coffee then?

GIL: If you're making some.

THEA: So why anaesthesia?

GIL: Well, you don't have to wear a tie.

THEA: Seriously.

GIL: When I was training, seemed like all the happiest people in the canteen were the anaesthetists. They got to go home while the others had to do ward rounds, sort out prescriptions, clinics, all on top of no sleep. And anaesthesia works. I like that.

THEA: You didn't want to be a surgeon?

GIL: No, I'm a born sidekick. You still haven't told me what you actually do at the prison.

THEA: Oh. Haven't I?

GIL: No. Are you something shameful? Is there something I don't know about prisons? Are you the executioner or something?

THEA: … I'm the chaplain.

GIL: You what! You *cheat*! You let me ramble on about God and the Bible! You must have been sniggering up your cassock sleeve!

THEA: I don't wear a –

GIL: I never knew chaplains could be such liars.

THEA: I didn't lie! Anyway I think I'm giving it up.

GIL: Why?

THEA: Crisis of faith.

GIL: Oh. You don't have to tell them that.

THEA: That wouldn't be very ethical.

GIL: I bet you could still help people. You're a good person.

THEA: Oh. No. I'm not that.

GIL: So… what on earth made you call me?

THEA: That was more to do with *you* being a good person. I told you, I wanted to thank you. For being inexplicably kind. And you made me laugh. Or smile, at least. It was the only relatively normal conversation I'd had in weeks.

GIL: The bubble.

THEA: Yeah. The bubble… You're supposed to ask.

GIL: What?

THEA: Why hadn't I had a proper conversation in weeks. You've asked me so many searching questions, but never stuff like that. You always change the subject.

GIL: I thought… if there was something, you'd tell me when you were ready.

THEA: And when I said I was divorced, you never asked if I had kids – even when I asked you.

GIL: Well – do you?

THEA: You really don't know?

GIL: Tell me.

THEA: I feel like everybody knows. I can't believe it when I meet someone who doesn't know.

GIL: Know what?

THEA: I lost my daughter. My nearly-sixteen-year-old daughter, Sam, three months ago. She took her own life.

GIL: Oh Thea I'm so sorry

THEA: And it was my fault. I mean, *really* my fault. I'm under investigation. She was slipping away from me, she was…

GIL: Go on.

THEA: It was always just me and her, and we were always… but then… I guess it happens to everyone, but first the hugs stopped, and then – I don't know, that's teenagers, isn't it? And then smartphones – she was the last of her friends to get one, the things terrified me – and for good reason. Seemed like the second she got it I was hearing about… 'The chaplain's daughter.' And every time I took it away, she'd promise not to do it again, but she would, she would do something worse, time after time after… So I went online myself, looking for answers, looking for guidance, and I came across this *community* – there was video after video of parents making their kids hold up signs with confessions on, or making them wear humiliating outfits, or cutting their hair off. As a lesson. There's a whole movement, a whole school of discipline and I – I just thought, that's it. I've been doing it all wrong, I'm a lazy first-world liberal, trying to be her friend, I need to 'be the parent', I need to take control, I felt so… exhilarated, so optimistic, like somebody had handed me the definitive answer.

She never even tried to fight when I cut her hair off. Even that made me think I was doing the right thing. I videoed it on her phone, for her to keep as a reminder – but I didn't post it online. Still don't know how it got there. But I know I killed her, Gil. I was seduced – I was trying to be something I wasn't, I thought I could protect her – but I was stupid and wrong and *bad*. Probably still am. And I got my punishment.

Silence.

GIL: What kind of daughter was she?

THEA: What?

GIL: Sam. What was she like?

THEA: That's not what people ask.

GIL: Sorry, would you rather not –

THEA: No, it's just people – if they don't already know, they always say 'Why did she do it?'. And if they do already know, they don't talk to me at all. Nobody ever says 'What was she like?'. She was… She had this little pixie face, even when she stopped being cute. And she liked ice cream sundaes and *The Wiz*, although in recent times I could never get her to admit to liking anything. And I wanted to hold her *all the time*, even though she never seemed clean. She was always either in her pyjamas looking about ten, or crusted with makeup looking about thirty. When she was little, she had this weird way of

crawling, I nearly took her to the doctor's, I thought there
was something wrong with her. Instead of using her hands
and knees she used her hands and one knee – she used to
shuffle herself around, drag her bum along –

GIL: What do you mean, hands and one knee? That doesn't
make sense.

THEA: Like this –

She demonstrates.

All her little trousers had a hole in one knee but not the
other, it was mad. She never did learn to crawl properly,
she went straight from this to standing.

GIL: Show me again?

THEA: Like this.

He tries it.

GIL: This has got to be the most inefficient way of getting
around anybody ever invented.

THEA: I know! Why do it the easy way when you can do it
your own way?

*They shuffle about for a moment, giggling at first and then collapsing
into hysterical laughter. For THEA, it's laughter verging on tears.*

Suddenly, she's kissing him. He responds. Then stops her.

GIL: Thea.

THEA: Gil, I need this.

They kiss again.

GIL: Thea. Please.

THEA: Let me have this, I need to feel something other than
pain, *please…*

She's grabbing, pounding at him.

GIL: Thea. I want to, but Thea… Thea!

He holds her at arm's length, looks at her.

I was there.

THEA: What?

Where? You were where?

GIL: I'm sorry. When Sam fell. I was… I was there.

THEA: When she… What? What the fuck are you saying?

GIL: It was… I'm sorry, I… It was my car she fell onto, when she jumped off the bridge. I… I could've died too, I was / this close –

THEA: What are you doing here?

GIL: I… had to find you… I didn't realise

THEA: Get out.

GIL: Let me talk to you Thea, it's / complicated

THEA: Get out.

GIL: I know I've gone about this all wrong, / I didn't know

THEA: GET OUT OF MY FUCKING HOUSE! You're sick! You're sick! What are you doing in my house? Get out get out get out get out get out get out

SCENE EIGHT

*Garden of remembrance at the crematorium. Halloween. BILLIE, dressed
as a sexy Scarecrow, skates in with LENNY, in a very cool Lion costume.*

BILLIE: He can't throw out mourners. *We* are what this place
is *for.*

LENNY: If you'd've just worn a coat!

BILLIE: Misogynist dress codes, Lenny, perpetuate rape
culture. Anyway. No one here to be offended.

LENNY: Let's just find her grave and get out of here.

BILLIE: No rush, the party's not for hours.

LENNY: You're mental. You completely ignore Sam's
sixteenth birthday, and then you pick tonight to visit her.

BILLIE: ''Tis the night – the night
Of the grave's delight,
And the warlocks are at their play;
Ye think that without,
The wild winds shout,
But no, it is they – it is they!'

LENNY: I'm going to delete that fucking app from your
phone.

BILLIE: I'm just saying. Now's the time the dimensions
overlap. That's why we leave out lanterns – so the dead
can find us, talk to us.

LENNY: So why couldn't we just put a pumpkin on the
doorstep and let her come to our place?

BILLIE: We won't be in, will we? She's not going to come to
Jude's, they hated each other's guts.

LENNY: Just don't start reciting spells and shit.

BILLIE: What, like 'St Nicholas of Tolentino, light the lamps. St Christopher, light the lamps. With the permission of the Iao Sabaoth, we make safe and sacred this space that we may traffic with the Honoured Dead. Beloved St Nicholas of Tolentino, shepherd my guides and helping spirits to this place...'

LENNY: Shut up.

Shut up!

Shut the fuck up, Bill!

LENNY: Do you remember when I stopped hitting you 'cos I got so big and you stayed so shrunken?

BILLIE: Well. You *said* that was the reason.

LENNY: Yeah well I'm about to change my mind.

BILLIE: Just be ready for me to bite you.

LENNY: You're not even human, are you?

BILLIE: So where are the graves, anyway? Is this even the right bit?

LENNY: I can't see one gravestone.

BILLIE: This is giving me the creeps.

LENNY: Billie.

BILLIE: What.

LENNY: ... Was she even buried?

BILLIE: What you on about?

LENNY: I never asked, did you?

BILLIE's mouth falls open.

LENNY: We'd've stood round a hole if they were burying her, wouldn't we?

BILLIE: I dunno. Just thought that's how they do it now. The chapel, the curtain… oh yeah.

LENNY: You seemed to know a hell of a lot about it at the time.

BILLIE: General knowledge. I didn't know any of the details about Sam's specific post-mortem circumstances. Fuck. This is just a garden.

LENNY: Nice, though. Nice flowers and shit.

BILLIE: D'you think they just dump all the ashes here together, then?

LENNY: Maybe. Or maybe her mum took them home in a pot.

BILLIE: Oh, gross. We've both been there. Maybe she was sitting next to us on the kitchen counter and we never even knew!

LENNY: So we don't even know if she's here or not.

BILLIE: I wanted to tell her what Jude said about the party.

LENNY: What did she say?

BILLIE: She would've definitely invited Sam if she was still alive.

LENNY: That's a lie.

BILLIE: Yeah. Fuck this is freaky. Only reason all these plants and that look so healthy is that they've been fed with people's dead relatives. Even the grass, look how green it is. 'From my rotting body, flowers shall grow and I am in them and that is eternity.' Edvard Munch *(she pronounces it 'munch')*. I mean basically these plants are ninety percent dead human. It's weird.

LENNY lies on the grass.

LENNY: Well if they spread her all over, the way to speak to her is this. Sam? Sam, it's Lenny here.

BILLIE throws herself to the ground.

BILLIE: Me first. It was my idea.

LENNY: No. Talking to her like this was my idea.

BILLIE: But it was me that thought of coming here.

LENNY: Without actually checking that she's not in a jamjar in her mum's kitchen.

BILLIE: You're so disrespectful.

LENNY: I'm not the one with her dead friend's phone wrapped in a pair of fucking ASOS knickers.

BILLIE: What?

LENNY: Nothing.

BILLIE: Have you been touching my things?

LENNY: No.

BILLIE: What the fuck have you been doing in my knicker drawer, you perv?

LENNY: Looking for Sam's phone, what do you think?

BILLIE: She gave that to me, not you. What were you looking for?

LENNY: Just wanted to see what was on there, that's all.

BILLIE: But it's locked.

LENNY: Yeah. I found that much out.

BILLIE: You weren't wanting to delete anything, were you Len?

LENNY: Like what?

BILLIE: Like, um, 'UR a slut. We're finished.'

Silence.

LENNY: I didn't mean it.

BILLIE: Mister Model Boyfriend, hanging out with Sam's mum, giving her jewels, lapping up all the sympathy at school, all the girls giving you pity hugs – judging me, judging her mum, acting all tragic and superior –

LENNY: Bill… Everybody was talking about the pictures she posted, calling her a sket, asking me why I was… They was all laughing at me. I really liked her, but she… They was nasty, them photos. Showing everybody things I hadn't even seen.

BILLIE: You really hadn't? That was just jokes when I said that.

LENNY: No. I really hadn't, all right?

BILLIE: But she was well up for it!

LENNY: Well maybe I wasn't! Maybe I wasn't ready. I don't think… I'm not sure I ever really knew Sam, Bill.

BILLIE: Are you gay, Len?

LENNY: Just 'cos I didn't have sex with Samantha Wilder, doesn't mean I'm gay!

BILLIE: It'd be all right if you was. Just for future reference. So. What makes you think you didn't make her commit suicide?

LENNY: Nobody knows what made her commit suicide!

BILLIE: I thought you said it was her mum?

I think we'd better leave, don't you?

LENNY: Thought you wanted to talk to Sam.

BILLIE: Nah. Not with you here.

LENNY: You want me to leave you here on your own?

BILLIE: No. Just don't know why you came. You think she'd want you here, after what you did?

LENNY: I'm sorry.

I'm sorry, Sam.

BILLIE: She's not here, you baby. She's *not here.*

SCENE NINE

GIL's flat. The lights are off. GIL lies on the couch eating a massive tub of sweets.

There's a loud knocking at the door.

GIL: *(Still eating.)* I haven't got any left! … Go away!

The knocking continues.

I've run out of sweets! … Bugger off! … No more –

He pours the sweets into a fruit bowl on the table, takes the empty tub to the door.

Look! Now will you FUCK THE FUCK OFF!

He opens the door. It's THEA. *Her hair is much shorter. They stare at each other.*

THEA: *(Turning to leave.)* D'you want me to?

GIL: No.

He lets her in.

You look different.

How did you find me?

THEA: You mentioned this street. I've been loitering with the helicopter mums, watching to see who opens the doors to the trick-or-treaters.

GIL: It's all your fault.

THEA: My fault?

GIL: Ever since you got me onto ice cream sundaes, I've had this raging sugar addiction.

THEA: So the sharing got too painful?

GIL: They're a load of greedy little shits. And not so little – some of them are taller than me. It's basically slow-motion looting. We'll have to keep the lights off, or I'll get eggs chucked at my windows.

THEA: Kids.

A sad and awkward pause. GIL *offers her the sweet bowl.*

You sure?

He nods. She takes some.

GIL: I like your hair.

I was so stupid.

THEA: I just want to know why.

GIL: I'm not sure I know.

THEA: Well, you're going to have to work it out. 'Cos I came all the way here and stood out in the cold for a good forty-five minutes to ask you, so you've got to at least try. And if I'm going to help you with these sweets, I need something to drink.

GIL: Sorry.

He scrabbles around, finds some cans of Red Bull.

This do?

THEA: If it's all you've got.

GIL: Thing is, Thea. I can't talk to you about... How can I talk to you of all people, about how it affected me?

THEA: Try.

GIL: Shit. This is...

I'm going to have to go back, to way before. You're going to have to bear with me, OK?

Another knock at the door.

FUCK OFF!

Look. There's a few things I haven't been honest with you about.

THEA: I worked that much out.

GIL: This place for a start. It's not some temporary pad I'm tolerating while my mansion gets remodelled. This is it. This is me.

THEA: But you're a consultant, you –

GIL: The business card. Yeah. That was me.

THEA: Was?

GIL: I figured it was unlikely you'd phone my work number. Just as well you didn't.

THEA: What happened?

GIL: Oh God. Not everyone deals with life crises as smoothly as you do, Thea. I had some stuff… nothing as major as… I should've coped, I should've… I dunno, cried more or binged on stuff like this and got fat. But I didn't. And look what was on hand in my daily job to help me through. I picked ketamine. Acts quickly, short half-life. Not as easy to get as it used to be, but it doesn't take much to get one step ahead of the paper shufflers. You get this, oh, people say it's like a Near Death Experience. It's like you're floating, you lose all sense of yourself, time stands still, it's… beautiful. And I was a doctor, how could I be…. I set up this elaborate cycle, gradually increasing the dose over ten days, always timing the peak effects for when I was off duty, have a couple of weeks' gap and then start again. And at first it didn't affect my work at all – and I never harmed anyone, even at my worst, but – Jesus, I ended up with my legs looking like mashed potato with swelling and ulcers and scar tissue and… My marriage was already wrecked by the time a colleague decided to confront me. They tried everything, they gave me a case supervisor and a psychiatrist… I could've kept my licence, I could've carried on, but I was still on my doctor pedestal, I reckoned I could handle it myself, wouldn't accept any help. So. Lost my wife, lost my job, lost my house – rock bottom as they say in the Steps. And now I drive for a living. Courier. Self-employed, supposedly. Barely earn enough to cover the rent on this toilet. Nothing spare for luxuries like insurance. And then…

THEA: Along came Sam.

GIL: Thea I can't –

THEA: Yes you can.

GIL: … The roof caved in about two centimetres from my head. She was that close to me for about half an hour. I drove on, with her up there –

THEA: You drove on?

GIL: Not – No, I let the car kind of drift to a stop. I don't know what I was thinking, I guess I didn't want to stop dead in the middle of a motorway. I suppose… I was trying to be careful with her. And then I sat there, and there were car horns blaring and cars going past and then I think some stopped alongside me and people were trying to help, but I just sat there for what seemed like forever, just breathing in and out and staring ahead and trying not to think about what was on the roof, what was *right there*, till the ambulance came.

THEA: *(Tears silently streaming.)* She nearly killed you.

GIL: I'm not – that's not what I'm saying.

THEA: She did, though.

GIL: It was just – in the weeks after, it was… kind of important for me to get back to work. For the money, to survive, but also for my, you know. My recovery.

THEA: And your car was written off. You must've hated Sam.

GIL: No. No. I never hated Sam, you have to believe me on that one.

THEA: But you came looking for me.

GIL: You do know how much there was online about you.

THEA: That's why I get human hair dumped on my – oh. You were part of that tribe.

GIL: No. I don't know any of them, I wasn't part of anything, I just… They were talking criminal charges –

THEA: Still are.

GIL: People were telling me to sue you, to go after you for the money –

THEA: That's what you were after?

GIL: Everyone was saying you were this…

THEA: Monster.

GIL nods.

GIL: It was a stupid idea. And then… there you were. Not a monster. And everything went out the window. And since then, I – I've been making enquiries about going back to work, proper work… You said that thing about *really living*, and I thought what am I waiting for? And I know it was so wrong of me to come into your life the way I did but it was so hard to tell you and now I'm just finding it… quite hard to be without you.

They stare at each other for some time, then they are kissing again with urgency and hunger.

SCENE TEN

THEA's house, the following morning.

THEA comes in, still in the same outfit but now extremely tousled. She goes to run a bath, returns, takes off her jacket. Finds a sweet wrapper in her pocket. Contemplates it.

BILLIE: *(Who's been motionless on the sofa all this time.)* Where have you been?

THEA jumps out of her skin.

THEA: JESUS CHRIST! Where the hell did you come from?

BILLIE: Sorry sorry sorry. Mum's spare keys. I rang the bell first, I've got manners.

THEA: Shouldn't you be at school?

BILLIE: Yeah. I got here really early. Plan was, I was going to have breakfast here and still get there on time. Did you even sleep here last night?

THEA: None of your business, Billie. Get to school. Come round later if you want to talk to me.

BILLIE: Sorry I scared you, but there's something I need to tell you and if I don't tell you now I'm going to lose my nerve.

THEA: Let me turn the water off.

She disappears briefly, returns.

BILLIE is holding Sam's phone.

THEA freezes, stares, then grabs it from BILLIE.

You know the police were looking for this?

BILLIE: Yeah, I know.

THEA: Why didn't you tell me about it before?

BILLIE: … I… I've only just found it.

THEA: What?

BILLIE: My room's a bit of a tip – worse since Sam died. I'd forgotten I had it.

THEA: Have you looked at it? Is there anything on there?

BILLIE: Um, yeah. There's something I think you should see.

54

She takes the phone back from THEA, taps, hands it back.

THEA reads.

She has to hide the fact that this finally breaks her.

BILLIE: I mean it's good news, in a way, isn't it?

THEA: What?

BILLIE: It wasn't your fault. She didn't do it because of you. After all. That's good. Isn't it.

I brought it 'cos I thought it might make you a bit... less sad.

THEA: Thank you.

I mean...

Why did she give this to you?

BILLIE: She just asked me to look after it, the day she... I mean she didn't say why.

THEA: And you didn't ask.

BILLIE: I was in a hurry, / I was

THEA: Right. But why you?

BILLIE: ... Why not? I was her friend.

THEA: So why didn't she talk to you?

BILLIE: Oh God – she *did* talk to me. She told me... what you did.

THEA: But why didn't she tell you what she was planning to do?

BILLIE: I can't see inside her head. I don't know. I was there for her, I plaited / her hair

THEA: You plaited her hair, yep. Your claim to fame.

BILLIE: Look, I'm sorry I didn't give you / the phone earlier

THEA: It's just that you knew all along that she planned it, didn't you?

BILLIE: Only after I read that.

THEA: And she trusted you to give it to me.

BILLIE: I have given it to you.

THEA: This is *evidence*, Billie.

BILLIE: I know, I know, Lenny's already had a go at me about that.

THEA: Lenny's a good boy.

BILLIE: Really.

THEA: What did you think of Sam?

BILLIE: … I loved her, / she was my

THEA: Oh you lot chuck that word about on social media like it's nothing. Someone says your photo's pretty and you say 'LYSM!' like it means 'Thanks'. It doesn't. You haven't a clue, / none of you

BILLIE: I'm sorry, Thea, but that's not fair. You've got no right to have a go at me after what you did.

THEA: I'm sorry?

BILLIE gathers her stuff.

BILLIE: Nobody dares say it, not to your face, 'cos it's too awful to actually tell someone they did something so wrong when they're already being punished so bad, but it's not like you're the victim here. You go around in your dog collar looking all superior and quoting the Bible like you're so much better than the rest of us. You turn your nose up at my mum's cooking, you take jewellery off a naive teenage boy, you stay out all night having sex – sorry, it's obvious – I mean when you think about it, if I had to choose between you as a mum and jumping off a bridge, I'd do the same as Sam! You want to know where she's gone? Well wherever it is, she's free. She's free from *you.* So don't you start telling me I failed her as a friend, because whatever I was, I could never be as big a failure as you.

And your hair looks shit.

She leaves.

SCENE ELEVEN

THEA's house, a week or two later.

GIL and THEA, awkward. THEA holds a bottle of wine.

GIL: It's for you.

THEA: You don't drink, do you.

GIL: Not worth risking a new addiction.

THEA: Like the sweets and ice cream.

GIL: Like the sweets and ice cream. I'm sorry to barge in, I just wanted to share some good news. Been having trouble getting hold of you.

THEA: Sorry.

GIL: It's OK… Can I / maybe –

THEA: Oh God. Yeah, come in. Shall I… open this, or –

GIL: Yeah, that's what it's for! I'll have a glass of water or whatever you've got.

THEA: So, good news. Haven't had any of that for a while.

GIL: Well I mean, I haven't won the Lottery or anything but... oh God, it feels like I have.

THEA: Go on.

GIL: I heard back from the GMC – General Medical Council. They've had a look at my case, and according to them, I've been clean long enough to re-register, as long as I accept supervision and support and –

THEA: That's fantastic, Gil.

GIL: Yeah. It's a big deal. Beginning to feel like me again. And I've got you to thank.

THEA: You'd've done this sooner or later, with or without some throwaway comment from me.

GIL: No. You're wrong. And! The police have finally decided not to charge you!

THEA: For some reason.

GIL: A suicide note?

THEA: 'An act prepared within the silence of the heart.'

GIL: No, they didn't say that.

THEA: Camus.

GIL: You're not... I mean, I don't expect you to be celebrating, / but

THEA: I'm not celebrating. I'm not even sure they've made the right decision.

GIL: You can't say that.

Thea?... I've been wanting to see you. That night... I've no idea how you feel about it.

THEA: You know what? The GP said, anytime I see a new doctor from now on, I have to tell them I'm a bereaved mother.

GIL: A new…

THEA: It's part of my medical history. It's changed my physiology.

GIL: Yeah. They're probably right.

THEA: … It was what it was. That night.

GIL: I don't know what that means.

THEA: The bubble.

GIL: Oh.

He takes a moment to swallow the disappointment.

Thea, I'm really sorry I wasn't upfront with you. And I'm so sorry if I've made your life any harder than it already is. I'd like to be able to help you somehow.

THEA: Well. Maybe you can help me find the fucking corkscrew…

GIL leaps up.

GIL: It was on the sofa when I was here before. Could've been very nasty.

THEA: No no, it's definitely not there, it's over here somewhere.

GIL: Trust me, I've got a knack for finding things.

THEA: It's fine / just sit down

GIL: No, it's a talent, I can do this… Oh.

Under a cushion, GIL has found a tiny phial. He holds it up. THEA lunges for it, but he moves it out of her reach. He rummages again and finds a syringe.

THEA: I had them in my hands when you rang the doorbell.

I don't have to explain myself to you.

GIL: No, no you don't have to.

THEA: It's your fault, anyway.

GIL: This is my fault?

THEA: You put the idea in my head.

GIL: Nothing I told you about this stuff could possibly have made you want to try it.

THEA: … The NDE. Near Death Experience?

GIL: What, you think this is / going to

THEA: I read up about it. One in three chance of a proper k-hole.

GIL: There's probably also a one in three chance of permanently losing control of your bladder. Or ending up like me. Or actually dying.

THEA: So?

GIL: Trust me, you don't want to do this.

THEA: Trust me, I do.

GIL: Why?

THEA: *I need to go where she's been.*

GIL: She hasn't / been

THEA: I did this stupid thing on her birthday –

GIL: Oh / no.

THEA: No, not that. I mean, yes, I've nearly done that. Few times. But it doesn't make any sense to me. Not 'cos God doesn't like it, it's more that… I never feel sure it would answer any of my questions. I just want to know, I just… It seems wrong that she experienced something so huge, without me. Before me. Like if your kids had sex before you did.

GIL: Now that makes no sense.

THEA: Exactly. No, what I did was I tried to pass out. It's just another way of having an NDE. Got one of her friends – her boyfriend – to help me.

GIL: Didn't work?

THEA: Not for me.

GIL: For him?

THEA: He scarpered before I could ask him. Haven't see him since. Don't blame him.

GIL: You're not going to see her by taking this, you know.

THEA: Maybe not. But maybe I can get a sense of… something. Get a glimpse of the… yellow brick road.

GIL: Or maybe you need to let her go.

THEA: Why? What's the point of having children if you have to let them go? From the minute they cut the cord, it's one long process of letting go and I don't want to let her go, OK? You're not a parent so you don't know.

GIL: No, I don't. I shouldn't even be touching these.

THEA: Maybe you should go then. You weren't supposed to find it.

GIL: But I have now.

THEA: No. Don't make me responsible for some kind of relapse.

GIL: Why didn't you get powder?

THEA: That's what I thought I was getting. Didn't want to embarrass myself by asking for a refund.

GIL: And you reckon you can shoot up without anybody showing you how?

THEA: I don't know, maybe.

GIL: I should've walked away as soon as I saw this.

THEA takes it from him. They are close now.

THEA: You still can. You need to get your life back.

GIL: Better still, I should've flushed it.

THEA: It's mine and it was expensive.

GIL: Is this all you've got?

THEA: No.

GIL: How many syringes?

THEA: A whole pack.

Gil, no.

Gil.

GIL: Let me help you.

They kiss. Before they've even disentangled themselves, GIL has the bottle and syringe in his hands.

What drugs have you taken before?

THEA: None.

GIL: Oh come on. Not even a puff of weed? At college, or –

THEA: Literally about one puff. Coughed my innards up. No idea how to inhale. Not sure I wanted to get high anyway.

GIL: Why?

THEA: I'm a control freak. Didn't you know that?

GIL: So they say.

THEA: After Sam was born, they gave me gas and air when they were stitching me back together. Closest I've ever got. Even then, oh God *(she starts giggling)* the midwives laughed at me 'cos I was cackling my head off. I think they thought I was going for it big time. But it was the opposite. I couldn't stop giggling at the fact that even though this was pain relief for my poor shredded vagina, I kept thinking 'Better not breathe in too hard or I might lose control.' Might lose control! What the hell was I worrying about?

GIL: Mustn't have too much fun while they're sticking needles in your vagina. You ready?

THEA: Not really. Can I have a drink first?

GIL: Wouldn't advise it. Here.

He helps her inject. She flinches.

Don't worry, you won't feel anything in a second. I assume the rest's – yep.

He's found the remaining gear in the fridge.

THEA: Why don't they use this stuff for stitching women up? It's an anaesthetic isn't it? And a sedative?

GIL: We don't really know about the effect on breastmilk.

THEA: Why did I ever worry about any of that?

GIL: Any of what?

THEA: Quality of my breastmilk. Fruit and veg with every meal. No Frosties, no Cheerios, no white bread.

GIL: Thought you said you were a lazy parent?

THEA: Do your homework. Don't do social media. No telly on a school night. What was all that for? Why didn't I just say 'Go and fucking enjoy yourself the best and most dangerous way you can?' She and I could've sat here and shot up together, none of it would've mattered, would it?

He prepares to inject himself. She puts her hand on his arm.

No. Gil. This is just for me.

GIL: I can't let you go alone. Just once. Old time's sake. Then that's it for ever. No one's going to know.

Injects.

THEA: … How long?

GIL: Not long when you do it this way.

They wait.

You never asked me why I never had kids.

THEA: Not everybody wants them.

GIL: No.

I did.

I mean, I *wanted kids*. 'You're not a man until you're a father.' You know the way some women talk about… the emptiness, the *ache* of… That's how it feels for me.

THEA: Ahhh

GIL: Kicking in?

THEA: Mmmmm

GIL: I'm a true failure. Not 'cos of the drugs, not because of my car-crash career, but because the *one thing* I... And I had my chance. I did it, I created a life! But... the woman I got pregnant was... not my wife, so. She didn't want it, and I couldn't very well... My marriage only lasted a year after that anyway, so.

I was convinced it was a little girl. The mother, she... It was just a fling, it would never have... But she was red-haired, she had this long beautiful red hair, and every time I saw a red-haired baby after that... It was – Thea? It was *nothing like your loss.* But I felt like I'd killed my daughter. That's... that's the bit I didn't tell you, about how the drugs started.

You know... I don't think this really makes sense, but you know how we talked about praying? First time we met? Well it's mad but the night before it happened, the night before Sam... I did this... stupid prayer. I prayed for my daughter, my dead daughter, my baby. I prayed that... God... would find a way to get her to me. Somehow. And that was me without drugs! I prayed for my own little red-haired girl. And she was on my mind when... when I saw Sam falling –

THEA: *(Voice thick and slow.)* You saw her fall?

GIL: Before I reached the bridge, before she hit my roof, I saw this figure, this little girl with long red hair falling –

THEA: Sam didn't have red hair.

GIL: Um... yeah. She did.

THEA: Oh. Yeah. She dyed it. Yeah. How did I forget that.

GIL: This girl, falling from the sky and for a split fraction of a stupid fucking split second I thought –

THEA: You kept… You kept driving. Towards her.

You didn't stop.

GIL: I wasn't thinking, I was just watching her, it's not like… I mean if she hadn't hit my car

THEA: She'd've hit the road. She might've died instantly.

GIL: Then you wouldn't have got to say goodbye.

THEA: Saying goodbye was… not a *good* thing…

GIL: When I read about… you know, about her hair… I couldn't make sense of the long ponytail I'd seen when she was falling. I thought I'd seen a different child, I kind of clung on for days to the idea that somehow that was my child coming to me, out of the sky

THEA: The sky

GIL: And then I read you'd left one long piece of hair and her friend had plaited it. That's when the anger started. And that's when I came looking for you.

THEA: You were angry, I never knew / you were

GIL: But by the time I saw you…

THEA is twirling slowly.

THEA: Everything's slowing down.

GIL: You might want to sit…

THEA: You sit, I'm fine, I feel kind of… little. And my voice… I never knew I talked so slow. It's nice. Kind of sexy.

They sway together, becoming less coordinated.

GIL: Here we go.

THEA: Oh I know – music.

She fumbles with a pile of CDs, puts some music on.

Oh. God. Everything's so… metallic. Is this what I've been missing? What's going on what's going on what's going on what's going on

She slows down, arms floating.

Ahhhhhhhhhhhh

Whooooo can't feel my legs

GIL: Yessssssssssssss

THEA tries to reach GIL but sits down halfway. Giggles. GIL laughs too but stops before she does.

He strips off his top with some difficulty, and disappears into his own world. Curls up on the floor.

THEA still giggles occasionally, but mostly stares, slumped and open-mouthed, at all the amazing things going on in her head.

GIL breathes fast and shallow. Grunts, lies peacefully.

They are still. Time passes. The music pulses.

Then a ring at the doorbell. THEA stirs but does nothing. The doorbell sounds again and again. She attempts to crawl, but fails, wails in protest. There's a key in the lock.

BILLIE enters just in time for THEA to empty the contents of her stomach onto her shoes.

SCENE TWELVE

The following morning. BILLIE feeds Frosties to THEA, who's propped up on the sofa. THEA resists.

BILLIE: Old people should be banned from taking drugs. Just 'cos you smoked a few herbs in the swinging sixties, but there's drugs and there's drugs. You need to eat something then get to the hospital.

THEA: Hospital?

BILLIE: Yeah, when you've sorted yourself out. I thought you must like these, you've got about ten boxes, these and Cheerios. You know one serving has as much sugar as nearly three chocolate biscuits? They've had to start calling these 'adult cereal', you know, 'cos they're too toxic for kids.

Have some water then.

THEA: What did you say about hospital?

BILLIE: Do you *remember* last night?

THEA: Yes…

BILLIE: After you mashed up my sixty-quid Vans, I got an ambulance for your boyfriend. Just thought you might want to find out if he's dead or what. No?

THEA: Gil?

BILLIE: If you say so. I'll run you a bath shall I? You look like shit and you don't smell too good.

She disappears briefly into the bathroom.

When I saw you on the floor looking all spazzy, then your boyfriend all, well, *dead* –

THEA: *Gil's dead?*

BILLIE: Nah. Probably not. Sooner you get ready, sooner we can go and find out.

She gently steers THEA into the bathroom.

No no, leave the door open – Mum always makes me do that when I'm feeling dodge, so she doesn't have to mash up the paintwork if I drown in the bath. Anyway you've probably got razorblades and shit in there, I don't know what you're capable of now. I rang her, by the way. Told her I was staying over at Jude's, so you've got me for a few hours yet. Good job I brought those keys again last night. You could've choked on your vomit, and then you'd be even worse off than him.

THEA: *(Off.)* Billie, what happened to him?

BILLIE: *(Sarcasm.)* Well I'm not sure, but I think he *may* have injected something.

THEA: *(Off.)* I know, / but I mean –

BILLIE: I've told you, I don't know.

I found something out. You'll know this, being a vicar, but I didn't.

THEA cries out. BILLIE turns.

You all right?

She immediately covers her eyes.

Oh fuck.

THEA: *(Off.)* I'm just a bit dizzy.

BILLIE: So yeah. Religious studies. Theology. 'Thea-logy.' Only just thought of that. Did you think of that? 'Thea-logy'? Is that why you became a vicar?

THEA: *(Off.)* What?

BILLIE: There was this woman, Christina of Bolsena, you know about her?

THEA: *(Off.)* No.

BILLIE: Thought you would. Italian. Where she comes from, they still act out her martyrdom once a year. I've seen the photos – it's really hot, all these half-naked muscly blokes carrying this gorgeous girl around with blood coming out of her mouth and that. You all right in there?

THEA: *(Off.)* Yeah I'm OK.

BILLIE: She was a twelve-year-old virgin that converted to Christianity and smashed up all her dad's pagan idols, gave the broken bits of gold to the poor. And then when he couldn't get her in line, he tried all these different ways to force her. Just say 'Yeah' every now and again so I know you're still conscious. I don't want to have to look again.

THEA: *(Off.)* Yeah.

BILLIE: So she gets beaten, she gets crushed on a wheel, she gets thrown in a lake, none of it works. Everybody that tries to hurt her just ends up dead. They put snakes on her body, and she *breastfeeds* them – how mank is that? – so they cut her boobs off and a load of milk gushes out instead of blood.

Pause.

THEA: *(Off.)* Yeah.

BILLIE: They cut her tongue out, they put her in a furnace, they carry her naked through the streets – and after all that, at the very end, do you know what they do?

THEA: *(Off.)* Yeah.

BILLIE: What?

THE: *(Off.)* No.

BILLIE: *They cut off her hair.*

THEA reappears in a bathrobe, but still dripping and looking disorientated.

THEA: … You didn't get that from an app.

BILLIE: *(Fetching a towel.)* No.

She dries off THEA's hair, arms, legs. Dries between her toes to the tune of 'One two three four five / Once I caught a fish alive':

Bits, bottom and between your toes / That's where the fungus grows

Bits, bottom and between your toes / That's where the fungus grows

… You'll have to do the rest yourself.

THEA: I used to wear leggings like Sam's.

BILLIE: What?

THEA: The leggings she had on in some of those photos.

BILLIE: Oh right, yeah.

THEA: Mine had stirrups, that was fashionable then.

BILLIE: Oh no they're back, stirrup leggings. You wear the stirrups on the outside of your shoes. They get a bit minging by the end of the day.

THEA: We didn't wear sports bras without tops then, but we did wear boob tubes which were probably worse. My mum hated my leggings.

BILLIE: You probably looked all right in them back then.

THEA: I was wearing them on the bus one day and it was a crowded bus and I suddenly felt a hand, fingers between my legs.

BILLIE: Oh gross! I hope you decked him, whoever he was.

THEA: No, I didn't.

BILLIE: I'd've grabbed his hand and held it up and said 'Who does this belong to?'

THEA: I hope you will, when it happens to you. I froze. The only thing I'd ever been taught was to be polite, to be *nice*, and anyway I was *scared*. I waited for my stop and I got off and I didn't look back, I ran all the way home and got straight in the bath and even there he was with me, I hadn't even seen him but I could smell this aftershavey, blokey stink

BILLIE: Are you trying to tell me why Sam's photos upset you that much?

THEA: It happened to me whatever I wore. In the street, in the *library* one time. It was happening to everybody. Still is.

I violated her myself, didn't I.

BILLIE: Violated!

THEA: Sorry. I forget you're just a kid sometimes.

BILLIE: I'm not a kid.

I violated her too.

THEA: No, Billie, you were her best friend. You're right, you looked after her. I'll always be grateful to you.

BILLIE: I thought she was a slut.

THEA: What?

BILLIE: At least you were trying to protect her. I was just –

I shared the video.

THEA: It was you?

BILLIE: Thought she had it coming.

THEA: How did you get hold of it?

BILLIE: She sent it to me. I pretended I sympathised, all that… I sent it to Jude, told her not to pass it on. 'Course I knew what would happen. She'll have known it was me.

THEA: She didn't say?

BILLIE: Don't think she even blamed me. I think she blamed herself.

It's why I came over last night, to explain. I was never her friend. I was a bitch. I was… I was starting to feel so… You all made me feel so invisible.

THEA: Who's 'you all'?

BILLIE: Lenny and Sam and you and everyone.

THEA shakes her head, uncomprehending.

BILLIE: It was like, step by step, it was like, there was Lenny, shining in all the things I wanted to shine at: music, sport…

THEA: I didn't know –

BILLIE: Nobody knew. Lenny got so big, I couldn't even keep up with him. Nobody even believed we were twins any more. And then Sam got so pretty. She even dyes her hair red with some two-quid box from Superdrug and ends up looking like the hot girl from *Riverdale*. I mean, that was *my* thing. And from then on I was either Lenny's sister or Sam's friend, and it was… And then the two of them start going out together! It was like losing both of them at the same time, it wasn't fair!

THEA: And me?

BILLIE: You just… You were always what I wanted to be.

THEA: No. Definitely no.

BILLIE: You were! You were so… I couldn't work out how you knew so much. You always had some wise words from some book, all like photographed in your head, ready for broadcast any given moment. You're from another planet. It was like, in your different ways, you'd all ganged up to make me feel, like, about this big. So when Sam sent me that video of her being… humiliated, being you know, like that Saint Christina, de-… de-feminised or whatever… it was like a gift. That's what it felt like.

THEA: Billie?

BILLIE: Yeah?

THEA: I don't want to go to the hospital.

BILLIE: I can't go for you, I don't even know the bloke.

THEA: I'm not sure I do, really.

BILLIE: What was he doing dying on your floor then?

THEA: You said he wasn't –

BILLIE: Nah, they said he'll be all right. Eventually.

THEA: Either way, I've messed up his life. I've messed up another life.

BILLIE: We do drugs at school, you know. I mean we don't *do drugs*, fuck. Sorry. I mean I know why people take drugs. People my age take them 'cos they're fun.

THEA: Trust me. Whatever last night was, it wasn't fun. I didn't even go where I wanted to go.

BILLIE: Yeah because you, you and your bloke, you take them to escape something. Which is not surprising really, because by your age, there's loads you need to escape from.

THEA: No. That wasn't / what I was

BILLIE: You know, blaming yourself is about the most egotistical thing you can do.

THEA: Billie, / my head

BILLIE: 'Cos when you blame yourself for something someone else has done, you're saying you had all the control over what they did. And they had none. Which is a bit insulting, really. All that stuff you said about wanting to go after Sam, if you think about it, you're still looking for control. You can't just, you know, sit with the mess.

THEA: Where are you getting all this from?

BILLIE: Me.

THEA: You're weird, Billie. So is that what you do? Sit with the mess?

BILLIE: No. I've been holding my nose and pretending it's not there.

THEA: Right.

BILLIE: Shall we go? I reckon I've got about an hour before my mum starts texting me.

THEA: Yeah.

She doesn't move.

BILLIE: You'll need to put some clothes on.

THEA: Yeah.

Billie?

BILLIE: Yeah?

THEA: I think I might be pregnant.

SCENE THIRTEEN

The park, two months later.

Poppies grow around the bench, which has a shiny little plaque on it. LENNY (with a new image: quirkier and less generic) sits assembling his saxophone. GIL approaches.

GIL: Sorry / I'm just

LENNY: No, it's all right

GIL: Just looking at the

LENNY: Oh

He shifts to one side.

Sorry.

GIL: No, no.

Thanks.

He turns to go.

LENNY: It's brand new. Today.

GIL: Yeah, I read about it. Thought I'd come and see.

LENNY: Did you know her?

GIL: Oh no. No. You?

LENNY: My girlfriend.

GIL: Oh! I'm so sorry.

LENNY: Thanks.

We were kind of… on a break.

GIL: Oh.

Must have been a shock.

LENNY: Yeah.

I planted these.

GIL: Oh. They're nice.

LENNY: Can't believe they grew.

GIL: Can't believe the council let you plant them.

LENNY: Oh.

D'you think I need permission?

GIL: Expect so.

LENNY: Oh right. Expect someone'll mow them down soon then.

GIL: What was she like? Do you mind me asking?

LENNY: Sam? Um, she was nice.

GIL: What does that mean?

LENNY: … I don't know. It's just – how much have you heard about her?

GIL: A bit.

LENNY: A lot of people got her wrong. I think we all got her wrong.

So was you just curious or what?

THEA: *(Off.)* Gil!

She appears. She and GIL look at each other. LENNY looks from one to the other.

GIL: Sorry. Just came to see the plaque.

THEA: It's a public place.

LENNY: Hello.

THEA: Sorry Lenny. It's been a long time.

LENNY: *(Remembering with embarrassment.)* Yeah.

THEA: You've met Gil then?

LENNY: Yeah except –

THEA: *(To GIL.)* How are you?

GIL: Still alive.

LENNY is painfully uncomfortable. Gets his phone out.

LENNY: I think I'll go and see if she's got lost. Can you look after this? *(The sax.)*

THEA: Of course.

He goes.

I'm sorry.

GIL: What for?

THEA: Nearly killing you. And then not keeping in touch.

GIL: Yeah. Fair enough.

THEA: I did come and see you, in the hospital.

GIL: Yeah, they told me.

I know it would have been hard for you to go there.

THEA: Just wanted to be sure you were OK.

GIL: 'Ok' might be pushing it.

THEA: Alive, then.

GIL: They told me I've got a red-haired girl to thank. Guardian angel.

THEA: Oh. Sam's friend.

GIL: Oh. Right.

You wouldn't believe how much that messed with my head.

THEA: I never meant to get in the way of your…

GIL: I was stupid with how much I used. Convinced myself I was being kind, taking most of it myself, protecting you from the worst of it. That's the trouble with the addict brain. Not a hundred percent rational when triggered.

THEA: But if I hadn't triggered you…

Was it… a complete disaster?

GIL: … Well. Maybe I'll go back to work one day.

Did you find what you were looking for? In the k-hole?

THEA: Maybe if I'd had more.

GIL: You know, you never told me if you had a 'calling'.

THEA: What's that / got to do with

GIL: When you decided to become a 'servant of God'. What was that, was it…

THEA: I didn't have a… It was just a decision, it felt right at the time. I felt needed. God didn't speak to me from a burning bush or anything, I don't think that happens.

What?

GIL: Nothing.

I just…

That night, you remember when you put that music on?

THEA: Sort of.

GIL: It was like, I dunno, it's not like it was the *Ode to Joy* or something, but it was like… through the music… It was like this truth and kind of… peace, sort of coating my skin? Or coming out of my pores or something. It sounds abstract but it wasn't, it was concrete and physical and real and… I'm sorry it happened to me and not you.

THEA: That's not what I was looking for.

GIL: Might've helped, though.

Don't get me wrong, I'm not thanking you for the experience.

THEA: No.

GIL: But I'm not blaming you, either.

THEA: Thank you.

A beat.

GIL: I've missed you.

LENNY: *(Off.)* Found her!

He enters with BILLIE, minus rollerskate.

THEA: Oh… Billie! You're on two feet!

BILLIE makes a face.

Gil, this is Billie. Sam's best friend.

GIL: Oh.

BILLIE: You look a bit different.

GIL: *Oh.*

  Billie. Can I give you a hug or would that be weird?

LENNY: That would be well weird.

THEA: *(Stepping in quickly, producing a small box.)* Shall we just do this?

LENNY: Oh my days, is that Sam?

GIL: Oh God, is this some sort of

BILLIE: Yeah.   THEA: Not really.

GIL: I should go. I never knew Sam.

THEA: You did meet her, though. In a way.

  It's not a funeral or anything. Stay.

  I'm really grateful you're all here. It's been a lonely few months, and that's my fault, I –

  Anyway, thank you.

  Everybody ready? What shall we… Shall I…?

LENNY: On the poppies.

BILLIE: Wait, what… these can't be poppies, it's winter.

LENNY: Well… tell them that.

THEA: But aren't they evil, the poppies in *The Wiz*?

LENNY: Only 'cos they send you to sleep forever.

THEA: … Here we go then.

THEA empties the box over the poppies. They all step back quickly, taken by surprise by the way the ashes billow upwards before falling. They dust themselves down.

LENNY: Well that was… fucked up.

THEA finds herself laughing, and it infects the others in different ways.

GIL: Thanks for letting me be here for that. All of you. I'm going to go now, I've got a meeting to go to.

THEA: A 'Meeting' meeting?

GIL: Yep.

THEA: Good.

GIL: You can call me, you know. If you want.

THEA nods. He goes.

BILLIE: *(Indicating the sax.)* Where did that come from?

LENNY picks it up.

LENNY: JD didn't want it. The girl in concert band's not into boys.

THEA: You going to play something?

LENNY: Nah. Too rusty.

BILLIE: Go on.

THEA: Go on, Lenny.

LENNY: *(Embarrassed.)* Let me just – give me a minute.

He wanders off. Distant sounds of hesitant, tuneless scales.

THEA: Thanks for all the messages.

BILLIE: 'Sall right.

He seemed all right. Your bloke.

THEA: He is. Not my bloke though.

BILLIE: He owes me.

THEA: Yeah. So do I. And I owe him.

BILLIE: That's not a good reason to –

THEA: No.

BILLIE: Have you told him?

THEA shakes her head.

What you did, that night, you know that was risky, don't you? For the…

THEA nods.

Do you think he would want you to keep it?

THEA: I don't know. Yes. Maybe not for the right reasons.

BILLIE: And do you?

THEA: How can I…

After everything I've done, how can I…

I have to decide soon.

BILLIE: 'I ask what is involved in the condition I recognise as mine; I know it implies obscurity and ignorance; and I am assured that this ignorance explains everything and that this darkness is my light.'

THEA: Is that –

BILLIE produces THEA's copy of The Myth of Sisyphus.

Thief!

BILLIE: It's not as hard as you made out.

THEA: Did I?

BILLIE: Thing is though, I did some googling and I'm not sure he was an atheist, you know. He asked some bloke to baptise him before he got mashed up in that car.

THEA: Well. What did he know, anyway.

LENNY's sax squeaks.

I thought you said he could play?

BILLIE: Yeah well. Like you said, he's a good boy.

The two sit together as LENNY's music coalesces and gains momentum.

BILLIE begins to sing. It is beautiful and unsentimental.

THE END

Quoted Poems and Texts

John McCrae, 'In Flanders Fields' (1915)

Albert Camus, *The Myth of Sisyphus,* 1942 (translation copyright 1955 by Justin O'Brien), published by Penguin Books

Charles Bukowski, 'Beasts Bounding Through Time', from *You Get So Alone At Times That It Just Makes Sense,* 1986, published by Black Sparrow Press

Scripture quotations taken from the King James Bible, as well as The Holy Bible, New International Version® NIV® Copyright © 1973 1978 1984 2011 by Biblica, Inc. TM. Used by permission. All rights reserved worldwide.

Arthur Cleveland Coxe, 'Halloween, a romaunt' (1869)

9 781786 829672